Blockchain

Tatiana Gayvoronskaya • Christoph Meinel

Blockchain

Hype or Innovation

 Springer

Tatiana Gayvoronskaya
Hasso Plattner Institute for Digital
Engineering gGmbH
Potsdam, Germany

Christoph Meinel
Hasso Plattner Institute for Digital
Engineering gGmbH
Potsdam, Germany

ISBN 978-3-030-61558-1   ISBN 978-3-030-61559-8   (eBook)
https://doi.org/10.1007/978-3-030-61559-8

This Springer imprint is published by the registered company Springer Nature Switzerland AG.
The registered company address is: Gewerbestrasse 11, 6330 Cham, Switzerland

Preface

Is blockchain an "alien technology" or a new encryption algorithm to achieve the creation of digital currency that has been turned into hype for marketing reasons? Technically speaking, blockchain is presumably a highly complicated, non-transparent technology, something that only corporate giants with innovation labs can work with – at least that is what most people think. The confusion is understandable, as even today[1] the debate rages on as to the "correct" definition of blockchain technology.

In 2016 and 2017, when the hype surrounding blockchain had reached its peak, numerous companies began to take part in the "blockchain experiment." Each had its own visualization of blockchain. This meant that the hype surrounding blockchain technology not only served to spur on development but, at the same time, was the most common cause of failure. The planning and development phases of numerous projects were shortened dramatically, so that the product could be brought to the market as quickly as possible and thereby profit from the extensive hype. At the same time, many technical concepts and projects that had already existed before the appearance of blockchain technology (and had little to do with its innovation) could be sold more successfully under the blockchain name. That the strongly hyped blockchain technology was met with disappointment should therefore come as no surprise. Looking at a new technology realistically is the cornerstone of its success. This can only happen when the innovation is used correctly.

In this book, we focus on the innovation of blockchain technology and the advantages this technology offers us when compared to existing solutions. Our goal is to provide a clear and comprehensive overview of blockchain technology and its possibilities, thereby helping you to form an opinion and draw your own conclusions.

Right from the start, we would like to sharpen our focus on the main objective of blockchain technology. To do this, we begin in the first chapter with the topic of decentralized networks, familiarizing ourselves with their challenges and using

---

[1] At the time this book was written.

the example of an online trading platform. In succeeding chapters, we explain what blockchain technology is, where it comes from, and how it works. Before we take a closer look at technical questions, we will explore the necessary technical foundations. In this chapter, we examine individual approaches at the core of blockchain technology, and how they are composed. With the help of well-known examples, such as Bitcoin and Ethereum, we look at the architecture of blockchain technology and focus on the challenges facing it, such as those involving security and scalability. Subsequently, we discuss the options available when introducing blockchain technology. Among other things, we will target best-practice examples to get a better idea of what areas benefit from this technology.

Numerous examples and detailed explanations will accompany you throughout this book. It is our hope that by the time you have reached the end, you will be able to decide for yourself what is truly innovative about the blockchain technology and what is nothing more than hype.

This book builds on our Technical Report [25] and aims to provide a comprehensive overview of blockchain technology. In addition to the technical foundations, it aims to cover the big picture, from the idea of the Bitcoin system to the challenges facing blockchain technology and its alternatives.

We would like to thank Mr. Matthias Bauer for his linguistic support in the writing of this book. We also wish to thank Dr. Sharon Therese Nemeth for the translation of this book from the German language edition.

Potsdam, Germany   Tatiana Gayvoronskaya
August 2020   Christoph Meinel

Contents

Chapter 1
Introduction

Abstract It is very comfortable to have an intermediary, such as a bank, who is able to intervene in sensitive matters and can control money transfers and account access. Also digital services like social networks, online trade or cloud storage provide us with access to an online platform and act as an intermediary between us and other users, service providers or an infrastructure. We usually pay with our data for the online services we get for free. The dissolution of the mediator also means the dissolution, or division, of the trust, management and resources among all users involved. Who then protects us if one of our communication partners turns out to be a fraud? Trust is a central issue in P2P networks. In this chapter, we would like to introduce you to the topic of decentralized networks and also to their challenges using the example of an online trading platform.

An unexpected situation suddenly arises. When transferring a large sum of money, you entered an incorrect account number. Panic sets in – what should you do now? Probably the first thing that comes to mind is to report what's happened to your bank. As your bank regulates all your transactions, it can easily track everything that has transpired and, in your case, reverse the transaction in question. It is comfortable to have a mediator, such as a bank, who can intervene in such matters and control the money transfer as well as access to your account. At the same time, as we have already seen, the price for this comfort is at the risk of your data becoming transparent and accessible for third parties. Continuing with the bank example, let us look at other online services, such as social networks, online trading or free cloud storage. The service provider makes an online platform available to us and acts as a mediator between us, other users, other service providers or an infrastructure. We usually pay with our data for services that we get online for free.

With the advent of the new General Data Protection Regulation (GDPR, in German DSGVO), we expect service providers to tell us what happens to our data; for instance, whom our data will be passed on to. Trust in the mediator, in our case the service provider, is "high," because we entrust him with our personal data. This concept is based on a kind of "network monarchy": the so-called client-server

© Springer Nature Switzerland AG 2021
T. Gayvoronskaya, C. Meinel, *Blockchain*,
https://doi.org/10.1007/978-3-030-61559-8_1

model. The name already gives us a picture of how the model works: you (the client) can obtain specific services by making a request for the service (at its server).

A dissolution of the mediator necessarily means the dissolution or the division of trust, management and resources among all parties involved. A so-called network democracy is then the consequence, which is also known as a decentralized network or peer-to-peer model (P2P). In such a network model, the parties involved take the place of the intermediary or in our case the service provider. This means that all parties who interact with each other in the framework of a service (e.g., you and the one to whom you want to transfer a sum of money) are simultaneously service users and service providers. The question then arises as to who is now responsible for the smooth workings of the service. For example, what if the party to whom you address the transfer is a new IT provider from abroad, whom you selected based on good Internet reviews, but with whom you have not had any contact to this time. To put it bluntly, you don't really trust the other party. So, who will protect you if there is a scammer hiding under the mask of the IT service provider?

1.1 Trust

Trust is a central issue in P2P networks. Without a so-called trusted third party, the users of a service are forced to either trust each other or to trust the system offering the service. It is possible to handle this situation in different ways. Building mutual trust could mean making use of the services dependent on certain conditions. For instance that you and your communication partner carry out a video identification process whereby you disclose your private information. This is, however, time consuming and does not offer protection from fraud. Another option is to build a trust network. For example, you are convinced of the professional competence of a colleague and therefore feel certain that the service provider he recommends will fulfill its promise. In this case, your participation in the system and the use of the service are similarly subject to conditions – you must have someone in the system whom you trust and who trusts you. Another way to build trust between parties in a decentralized system is to engage in a mutual evaluation of the behavior of all participants. In such a reputation-based system, participants can simply join or leave the system at will since their participation is not subject to any conditions (permissionless system). An example of a reputation-based system is the trading platform eBay. However, to eliminate the opportunity for malicious users to give other users false ratings, a decentralized system of this kind must be subject to further restrictions.

1.2 Resource Allocation and Administration

Let us continue with the example of the online trading platform. The only difference now is that we do not have a central authority through which all queries go and to whom we can report a malicious user. We want to now use a decentralized system in which users do not trust each other because they do not know each other. Furthermore, they do not have to fulfill any other conditions (permissionless system) to join the system and to use the service other then installing the app. In this case, it would help us if certain system rules were in place that all users had to follow. At the same time, it would be wrong for us to assume that all users act rationally and follow the set rules strictly. For this reason, we would like to use the best-known behavior control measures – reward and punishment. In practice, this means that all users in our system are rewarded if they follows set rules, just as they are punished if they violate the rules.

If the punishment is not a sufficient deterrent, malicious users will still try to get around the rules and to manipulate our online trading platform. For example, for such a user it is more worthwhile to sell one expensive TV multiple times and subsequently have his account blocked when found out, and after that to establish a new account, as to get a reward for being "honest" at half the price of the TV. Since all users in our system are at the same time service providers, all follow the same rules and have the same rights, all the resources (data on the products, communications, transactions, etc.) are distributed to all users, verified by each user and then saved. If such a malicious user sells the same product multiple times[1] and the information on every sale (more specifically, the transaction) is spread to all other users, they will then identify the fraud. However, if the malicious user floods our online trading platform with numerous false identities (also known as a Sybil attack), it will be hard for honest users to establish the truth. In this case it is important that honest users make up the majority.

How large the majority must be was a question that had already occupied scientists in the 1980s, as seen in the work by Leslie Lamport, Robert Shostak and Marshall Pease [19]. These scientists described a tolerable ratio of malicious users to honest users in a decentralized system.

The problem of finding a consensus in a decentralized network (i.e., in spite of the contradictory informations/statements by malicious and honest users in reaching an agreement) has become known as the "Byzantine Generals Problem" (see Sect. 3.3).

The more malicious users a decentralized system is able to tolerate, the more robust it must be. Historically-speaking, such systems have been linked to a number of conditions (permissioned systems), for example whether the number of system users and/or their identities are generally known. In decentralized systems, such as the Internet, such conditions would be inefficient as well as nearly impossible to fulfill. In contrast, the Nakamoto consensus mechanism, which is anchored in

---

[1] Also known as double spending.

blockchain technology and was used for the first time in the Bitcoin system, also works in networks that do not place restrictions on the number of system users or on identifying them (permissionless system). This means, users are free to join and leave the network as they choose [24].

In fact, the Nakamoto blockchain protocol is explicitly designed to work in a network with message delays, and is in fact used in just such a network (the Internet) [28]. This protocol contains several rules/algorithms that ensure the security of blockchain technology against manipulation.

With this book, we would like to help you in forming your own opinion about blockchain technology and thus be able to distinguish between what is truly innovative about blockchain technology and what is nothing more than hype.

Chapter 2
What Is Hidden Behind the Term "Blockchain"?

Abstract We now know about the basic challenges facing the secure use of decentralized systems, and, by way of an example, have seen what has made blockchain technology possible. Before we dive deeper into the subject matter, we will attempt to gain a better understanding of blockchain technology by way of a previous example. We also want to draw a demarcation line between the terms Bitcoin and Blockchain.

2008 is considered to be the year of blockchain technology's birth. Satoshi Nakamoto laid the cornerstone for blockchain technology in November 2008 with the publication of "Bitcoin: A Peer-to-Peer Electronic Cash System." And already in January 2009, he published the first version of the Bitcoin open-source software.

The identity of Satoshi Nakamoto remains a mystery. The name has long been suspected to be a pseudonym behind which a group of developers is hiding. In 2008, the Bitcoin system was intended to revolutionize the financial sector – hard hit by the financial crisis – and to offer a third-party independent, digital payment system. The cryptocurrency called bitcoin was created as a digital currency based on a decentralized and cryptographically secured system of payment.

> What is needed is an electronic payment system based on cryptographic proof instead of trust, allowing any two willing parties to transact directly with each other without the need for a trusted third party [26]. – Satoshi Nakamoto

The idea of a secure decentralized payment system already existed before Bitcoin came along. However, none of the proposed approaches could prevail due to errors either in the concept or because of problems with security.[1]

The blockchain technology on which the Bitcoin system is based, on the other hand, enables a robust and secure decentralized system, without any precondi-

---

[1] Such as the problem of double spending the same money (double spending problem – this would be as if a banknote were copied and then issued/spent in duplicate form) and lack of security to protect against a Sybil attack (in such an attack a malicious user assumes any number of false identities) etc.

© Springer Nature Switzerland AG 2021
T. Gayvoronskaya, C. Meinel, *Blockchain*,
https://doi.org/10.1007/978-3-030-61559-8_2

tions placed on the number of system users or their identification.[2] Simultaneous protection is provided against Sibyl and double spending attacks [28]. The terms Blockchain and Bitcoin are often incorrectly used as synonyms, whereby Blockchain is a technology and Bitcoin a concrete system that uses Blockchain technology for digital payment processing.

Because the implementation of the Bitcoin concept is open source, it is possible for anyone to use the code for their own blockchain application and to adapt it accordingly. The term blockchain first came into being following the creation of new bitcoin-like projects, when it was necessary to make a conceptual distinction between these and the already existing Bitcoin system. In later years, other terms have become prevalent such as distributed ledger technology, which refers to the most widespread use case of the blockchain technology: the so-called decentralized "registry." [24]

In the meantime, numerous projects have arisen that are based on blockchain technology and offer a large variety of services and products. Thus, the implementation of blockchain technology is not just limited to the area of cryptocurrency or decentralized registry, but the technology is used to a great extent as a programmable, decentralized trust infrastructure [192] – so-called Blockchain 2.0 (see Sect. 4.1.1). This is based on a further development of the original concept of blockchain technology, which now offers not only a robust and secure decentralized system for value exchange or logging[3] (registry), but also enables digital autonomous contracts (so-called smart contracts).

So what is behind this new registry or trust infrastructure, and how can we use it in concrete terms? Is it a magic bullet for our problems or just a new, unnecessarily complicated web of computer science that the media have discovered for themselves and turned into hype?

2.1 Understanding Blockchain: A Simple Example

Let us consider blockchain technology using the example of the decentralized online trading platform that was previously described. In this instance we already have a decentralized system with numerous users spread all over the globe. The users neither know each other nor do they trust each other. Our users do not have to meet any conditions to join the system. To use the system, they only need to install the corresponding app. Since all users of our system are simultaneously service providers, and all have the same rights, all resources[4] and the administration[5] of the system are allocated to every user. These are available to users via the app. To

---

[2]Users are free to join and leave the network as they choose (permissionless system).

[3]Information logging.

[4]Data on the products, communication, transactions, etc.

[5]Fixed regulations, verification of resources, establishing and managing of communication, etc.

put it more precisely, besides containing all rules and functions every app also has a database with an copy of all resources. For example, the sales advertisement you have just created is sent to all users in the system and stored in the database of each user.

In this way, all the users' apps communicate together. They all exchange data, check the data they receive and save it. Due to different delays, the data is distributed at different periods of time on the Internet. As we do not have a centralized service that records and manages the incoming data, we need an administration mechanism. It must include a tamper-proof time stamping service to ensure the correct and uniform order of information included in the system for all users. The following example gives us an illustration of this.

> Let's assume you sold your TV on our online trading platform. Your app creates a transaction with the sales data (e.g., sales object, buyer, price) and sends it to all users on your address list. The apps of these users verify the transaction sent from your app based on fixed rules. A copy of the transaction is also saved and forwarded to all users in their address books. In this way, your transaction spreads throughout the entire system. The buyer of your TV receives the transaction from one of the users who had his address in the address list. He carries out the same procedure in handling the transaction: verify, save, and forward. During verification, it is determined by the buyer's app that the transaction is addressed to him and he visualizes the contents of the transaction for the buyer in the user interface. Shortly after the purchase, the buyer of your TV decides to resell the TV. When he has found a buyer, he creates a new transaction and sends it out. Let us assume that your transaction has not yet spread throughout the whole network and a user receives the second transaction first. In this case, in the verification process he will declare that the transaction is wrong, because according to the information stored in the system (information in his app) the TV still belongs to you.

Blockchain technology uses cryptographic linking and a connection of contents (linked time stamping) in order to determine for all users the correct and uniform order of all the information included in the system. Because a decentralized system, whose users are not bond to certain conditions, can also attract dishonest/malicious users, the connection of contents is combined with a computationally complex task.

Blockchain technology assumes that in a system without conditions of participation (malicious users can generate many false identities) the majority of computing power is in the hands of honest users and not that the majority of users are honest. In this way, the robustness of blockchain technology is guaranteed [28].

Each user can thus provide a timestamp and thereby store the contents in a uniform sequence and spread it throughout the system. A reward serves as a motivation for users to perform a computationally demanding task and thus to ensure the security of the system.

This means that every user of our service is able to get a reward if he cryptographically links copies of the content distributed in the system and saved in his app (e.g., ads, transactions etc.). Our system would be far too slow if, every time new content arrives, our users were to solve a computationally complex task and would cryptographically link all contents individually with each other. To make the process more efficient, our user will first merge multiple contents[6] into a list of a specified size (Bitcoin 1 MB, Ethereum[7] approx. 27 kB) and create a cryptographic "fingerprint" of the list (Merkle root[8]). The fingerprint along with other metadata,[9] solution to the computationally complex cryptographic task and the "link" to the existing content[10] will be compiled in a list header. The list of the contents together with the additional information (list header), is called the `Block` in blockchain technology and the list header correspondingly the `Block Header`. The link to the already existing contents is nothing more than a cryptographic "fingerprint" of the block header of the previous block.

After a block is created, it is distributed to all users like the other content. Each user verifies the block it has received, adds its copy to the last block in its database and forwards it to the other users. Consequently, an ordered block chain is formed – and thus the term `Blockchain` was born. The content that has already been included in a new block is deleted from the buffer (memory pool) and remains saved in block form in the users' databases.

Since we have a decentralized system, it can happen that several users simultaneously solve the computationally complex cryptographic task and each create and distribute a new block with the same contents. If these blocks comply with all rules and refer to the same last block, it is possible that the chain will branch. This branching is also known as a `fork`.

The solution for this is at the same time the most important rule in a blockchain-based system: "The longest chain is valid because the workload there is correspondingly higher." This rule is also called the `Nakamoto consensus` (more in Sect. 3.3). Due to the network delay, it takes different time to spread the blocks. This means that the user who wants to create a new block, will link it to the block that he received first. The reward is paid out only to the user whose block is in the longest chain. Thus, after a time, only a single chain will prevail. The shortest chain is ignored; its blocks are called `orphan blocks` (see Fig. 4.6). However, the information contained[11] therein does not expire. What is not yet contained in the valid blocks, will be saved in the buffer (memory pool) of the user.

---

[6]Information, values.

[7]May 2020.

[8]More in Sect. 4.1.1.

[9]More in Sect. 4.1.2.

[10]Information, values that have already been stored in the database of the app.

[11]In the Bitcoin system, values in the form of transactions.

Thanks to cryptographically linked time stamping and the computationally-intensive cryptographic task, the plan of the malicious user to pocket the money for his television several times over will not succeed easily. In each of his fraudulent transactions, he assigns the same object (a television with a certain identification number) to a new owner/recipient, confirms the transaction with his signature and sends it to other users. Only one of the transactions will be included in a new block (the one that first arrived at the user who created the block). The others are declared void.

But if the malicious user had more computing power than all of the other users put together, he would be able to monopolize the creation of new blocks and in this way enforce his own blockchain, the longest chain. This approach is also known as the `51 percent attack`.

In this case, the malicious user can create a second transaction with the same product (the television that has already been sold to a user) and a new buyer. First, he waits until his first transaction has been included in a valid block and he has received the money for the sale. Then, the malicious user creates a new block containing the second transaction, and he distributes it throughout the network. In this case, it is important that the previous block of the first and the second transaction is the same. This creates a branching effect in the current, valid chain – a so-called `fork`. The malicious user must enforce[12] the new chain until it is longer than the other chain, and he subsequently receives money for his second transaction as well.

---

[12]By creating new blocks for it.

Such an attack would be nearly impossible in the Bitcoin system, as the level of difficulty of the cryptographic task is very high in comparison to other blockchain-based systems and consequently requires an enormous energy expenditure (see Sects. 3.3 and 4.1.3).

How these topics are related will be examined in the next chapters. Before we turn to the technical foundations of blockchain technology, we will take a brief look at the first blockchain application: the Bitcoin system.

2.2 Bitcoin

The term Bitcoin is associated with the first application of the blockchain technology – that is, a decentralized and cryptographically secured payment system.

Instead of using a so-called fiat currency[13] a digital currency is used, a so-called cryptocurrency named bitcoin (BTC[14]).

The blockchain technology, upon which the Bitcoin system is based, enables a robust, decentralized system without any requirements regarding the number of system users or their identification.[15] All users are simultaneously service providers. They have the same rights and the same copy of the database (public blockchain – more information can be found in Sect. 4.1.4).

This database can be compared to a public register or land register, made up of ordered and unchangeable entries that are updated by all users consistently based on a consensus (the longest chain is valid and means more effort[16]). In the Bitcoin system, for example, these registry entries represent transactions [28]. In the transactions, Bitcoin values (bitcoins) are transmitted between different addresses (comparable to a bank account number) or, more specifically, the addresses in the transactions will be renewed/overwritten.

Blockchain technology is often called the "Internet of Value" because in most applications the focus is essentially on the decentralized logging of the ownership of certain values. This means when a value was owned and by whom. In addition to cryptocurrencies, these values can represent securities, a rented apartment that changes its tenants, a kilowatt hour of solar power that is traded between neighbors, or the authorization to unlock an office door, which are then recorded in the blockchain "register."

Since the database is public this means that in the Bitcoin system, for example, information about who received bitcoins from who and how many is made public knowledge as well as the "account balance" and that all the transactions from an address[17] are traceable [52]. While the disclosure of all information helps to guarantee the security of the system (everyone is allowed to verify all contents) and a better scalability in relation to the number of system users (everyone can join or leave the system at will), it impairs the privacy of the users.

In order to disguise the identity of the users, many blockchain applications, including Bitcoin, use pseudonyms – so-called user addresses, comparable to a bank

---

[13]Fiat currency, or fiat money, is money that is not covered by any assets. The money is used as a medium of exchange, but has no intrinsic value. Today's currency systems are usually not covered by a commodity. For example, money issued by a central bank, such as euros or dollars, is called fiat money.

[14]BTC is the abbreviation of the Bitcoin currency. Bitcoin has several decimal metric units. For example, 0.1 BTC is a deci-bitcoin (dBTC), 0.01 BTC is a centi-bitcoin (cBTC), 0.001 BTC is a milli-bitcoin (mBTC), 0.000001 BTC is a micro-bitcoin (μBTC) and 0.00000001 BTC a Satoshi – the smallest possible unit.

[15]Users are free to join and leave the network at will (permissionless system).

[16]A computationally-intensive cryptographic task for each block in the chain.

[17]Comparable to a bank account number; more in Sect. 3.1.2.

account number – which are difficult to trace back to the end user (see Sects. 3.1.2 and 4.2). Besides pseudonyms, further concealment tactics are available for the Bitcoin system, for example:

- Use of the anonymous network TOR [183] for concealment of IP addresses,
- Anonymous mixing services (also called tumblers) are intended to conceal the receiver of the transaction. The bitcoins to be transferred are divided into several parts and sent to multiple addresses suggested by the mixing service provider. Subsequently, the same number of new bitcoins are then sent from these addresses to the actual recipient. This service naturally requires the trust of the user and is not legal in every country.

Just as many other currencies, bitcoins can be bought and traded via platforms in the Internet for a fee, for example through CoinBase, BitPay or AnycoinDirect. As the demand for bitcoins fluctuates strongly, the price is also dependent on the strong fluctuation. In the past, just in the time span of one week, the price changed by up to 25 percent. In recent years, the rate of the bitcoin has set new records. In December 2017, the value of a bitcoin (BTC) stood at EUR 16,000 for a short time, but fell to EUR 5,500 at the beginning of February 2018. In January 2019, a bitcoin cost approx. EUR 3,000 and in January 2020 the bitcoin rate exceeded the EUR 7,000 threshold.

The Bitcoin system ensures a constant inflow of new bitcoins. These are distributed as a reward in the context of block creation to the block creating users. In 2013, already 8 million bitcoins were in circulation and in June 2019 nearly 18 million. The upper limit set by Satoshi Nakamoto in the Bitcoin architecture of 21 million bitcoins will be reached to 99 percent in 2032 [39]. Endless inflation is prevented from occurring due to the defined upper limit of existing bitcoins [61].

In order to manage (transfer, receive, and store) bitcoins, the user needs a Bitcoin "wallet." Mobile, desktop and web applications are available for the wallet. There are also physical Bitcoin wallets, such as hardware and paper wallets[18] (Figs. 2.1 and 2.2). The cryptocurrency wallets analyze the blockchain and then, to give the user a better overview, display the user's incoming and outgoing transactions and current supply of money.

The Bitcoin currency is already accepted by many companies as a means of payment – from IT service providers to those companies in the gastronomy sector (see Figs. 2.3 and 2.4).

After this brief overview of blockchain technology and the Bitcoin system, we will delve deeper into the subject matter in the following chapters. To do this, let's first look at the basics necessary to understand blockchain technology.

---

[18]More on the subject of the hardware wallet can be found in Sect. 4.2.

Fig. 2.1 Hardware wallet Trezor One [186]

Fig. 2.2 Hardware wallet Ledger Nano X [151]

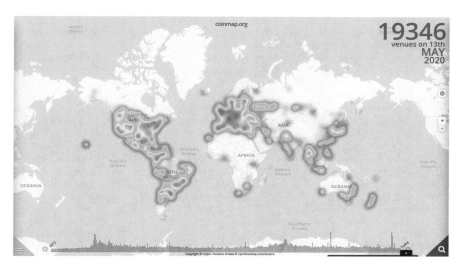

Fig. 2.3 Spread of the Bitcoin currency worldwide [99]

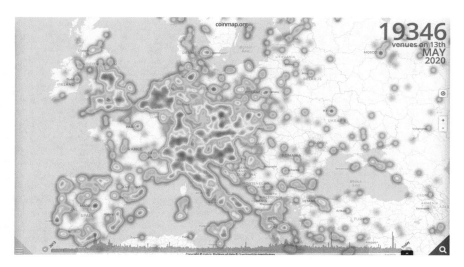

Fig. 2.4 Spread of the Bitcoin currency in Europe [99]

Chapter 3
Technical Basics for a Better Understanding of Blockchain Technology

Abstract The context for the subject of blockchain has now been established. Some readers perhaps may not have a technical background to allow for a complete understanding of the entire mechanism of blockchain technology. In this chapter, we would like to take a closer look at the individual approaches that make up blockchain technology and how they are composed.

The innovation of blockchain technology should neither be understood as a new encryption algorithm nor an "alien technology," but instead as a successful combination of already existing technological approaches, such as cryptography, decentralized networks, and consensus finding models.

In the following chapters we will look in more detail at these individual approaches and how they come together in blockchain technology.

3.1 Cryptography

The term cryptography comes from ancient Greek and means "secret writing" [147]. But it also describes the science that deals with the security of messages (encryption, decryption, checksums, etc.). The classic task of cryptography is to make a message incomprehensible for outsiders [3]. In the course of its long history[1] several approaches have been established in the field of cryptography. One of the most important developments in cryptography is Kerckhoffs's principle, which describes the transition of the secrecy of the algorithm to the secrecy of the key.

> The security of a cryptographic procedure is based solely on the secrecy of the key. – Kerckhoffs's principle [10, 16]

---

[1] Already 3,000 years before we began to calculate time, cryptography was used in ancient Egypt [147].

© Springer Nature Switzerland AG 2021
T. Gayvoronskaya, C. Meinel, *Blockchain*,
https://doi.org/10.1007/978-3-030-61559-8_3

15

In this way, an encryption procedure can be made public and examined for weaknesses by experts worldwide and improved. Kerckhoffs's principle is applied to the so-called symmetric-key algorithms (AES, DES, IDEA). Thus, a message is encrypted and decrypted using the same key. This means that the sender as well as the recipient must have the key. The problem is that the key must be kept secure, and at the same time it must be exchanged in secure way between the communication partners. This gets even more complicated if we want to have multiple encrypted communications. In this case, we would need a different key for each. The asymmetric-key algorithm stands in contrast to this procedure. Also known as asymmetric cryptography or public-key cryptography, it relies on a key pair – a key available to the public for encryption and a secret key for decryption.

In blockchain technology, digital signatures from the public-key cryptography and cryptographic hash functions from the checksum technique are used.

3.1.1   Digital Signatures and Hash Values

The basic idea in public-key cryptography is that all participants who engage in encrypted communication have a different pair of keys, instead of a common secret key, for encrypting and decrypting messages. Each participant has a secret key, also called a private key, and a public key. The public key is freely available to all communication partners. The secret key must – as the name suggests – remain secret and is used to decrypt and sign messages.

Let us consider an example with two interaction partners who we shall call Alice and Bob. Alice wants to send a message to Bob. Alice encrypts the message with Bob's public key before sending it. Only Bob is able to decrypt the message with his private key (Fig. 3.1) [11].

A digital signature is a number or a sequence of bits that is calculated from a message using the public-key procedure and whose authorship and affiliation with the message can be checked by anyone [12].

By signing the message, Alice confirms that it has actually come from her (she uses her private key to do this). Bob can confirm this by verifying Alice's signature using Alice's public key (Fig. 3.2).

Fig. 3.1 Public-key cryptography

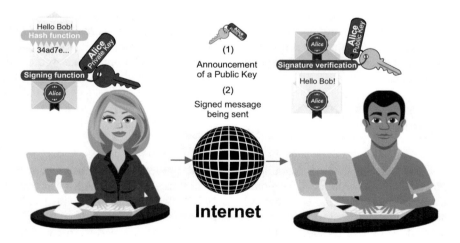

Fig. 3.2 Digitally signing and verifying a message

Hash functions are one-way functions. This means that the mathematical cal-culation is simple in one direction[2] but very difficult in the opposite direction,[3] if not nearly impossible [11]. A hash function converts an amount of data of various lengths into a hexadecimal string of a fixed length. The hash value consists of different combinations of numbers and letters between 0 and 9 and between A and F (as a substitute for the hexadecimal numbers 10 to 15). This procedure makes it possible to identify a message relatively clearly[4] and easily, without revealing the message contents. For this reason, the hash value is often called a fingerprint.

The most common hash function used in blockchain technology is SHA-256 (Secure Hash Algorithm), where 256 indicates the length of the hash value in bits. Even the smallest change to the message results in a completely different hash value. The following example shows the great differences in the SHA-256 algorithm hash values based on variations of the name Alice:

- Alice
  3bc51062973c458d5a6f2d8d64a023246354ad7e064b1e4e009ec8a0699a3043
- Alice1
  9d328d8b7ac56e1f71ce94ed3c7975d63c8b6f1a54d5186de8881cf27dd8b3a9
- alice
  2bd806c97f0e00af1a1fc3328fa763a9269723c8db8fac4f93af71db186d6e90

In blockchain technology, digital signatures are used to confirm that the trans-actions are derived from one's own resources. Since hash values allow a relatively clear and simple identification of the data, they are used as references in blockchain technology. For example, in the third Bitcoin block we find a reference to the second block. This reference is the SHA-256 hash value of the second block and looks like this: 000000006a625f06636b8bb6ac7b960a8d03705d1ace08b1a19da3fdcc99ddbd. Not only is an unambiguous identification and referencing of the blocks possible through this procedure, but it also ensures that the block contents are protected against manipulation.

3.1.2 User Identification and Addresses

For the purpose of user identification special pseudonyms are used in many blockchain applications. The pseudonyms are used simultaneously in many blockchain applications as "account numbers." They are therefore also called addresses (e.g., Bitcoin addresses). Originally in the Bitcoin system it was possible to send bitcoins to IP addresses [69]. However, this also opened up opportunities

---

[2]Calculating a hash value from a plain text message, for example from the name Alice.

[3]Calculating the original message only using the hash value and the hash algorithm.

[4]Collisions are very rate, but not unheard of. The collision resistance varies depending on the hash functions.

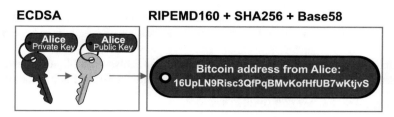

Fig. 3.3 Address generation in the Bitcoin system

for attack. In order to credit a user with a Bitcoin value, cryptographic methods are used exclusively in the creation of addresses. To make this possible, a cryptographic key pair is generated at the user.[5] The private key is used for signing transactions[6] (confirmation of ownership) and the public key is used for generating addresses.

The key pair is generated in the Bitcoin system, as in many other cryptocurrencies (e.g., Litecoin, Dogecoin, etc. [69]) with the ECDSA public key procedure (Elliptic Curve Digital Signature Algorithm) based on elliptic curves.[7] First the private key is generated, which represents a random number. The public key is derived from the private key and then "hashed."[8] In the end, the address is a 160-bit alphanumeric value (e.g., 16UpLN9Risc3QfPqBMvKofHfUB7wKtjvS). This is why such addresses are also called a "Pay To Public Key Hash Address" or a P2PKH address (see Fig. 3.3).

Some blockchain applications offer so-called multi-signature addresses. Several private keys are generated for this purpose [55] with the intention of increasing security. The recipient, who has received assets, must own all of the necessary private keys in order to use the assets that he has received. In a company that accepts bitcoins, multi-signature addresses can, for example, be used to confirm the expenditures of individual employees after the approval by controlling. In this case, both the employee and the controller each have their own private key for one shared Bitcoin address [63].

Since generally all information (in the Bitcoin system, e.g. transaction) are public in a blockchain[9] system for all users, it is always possible to track the previous owner (the P2PKH address) as well as the entire "history" of a value and to see all of the

---

[5]In his blockchain app.

[6]See Sect. 4.1.1.

[7]Explaining this exciting, but very complex, mathematical procedure would go beyond the scope of our intention here.

[8]To generate the address from the public key, two cryptographic hash function are used in succession on the public key (RIPEMD-160 and SHA-256) and the hash result is encoded according to the Base58 scheme (letters and numbers with the characters 0 (zero), O (capital o), I (capital i) and l (small L)).

[9]As applies to the public blockchain and the consortium blockchain (see Sect. 4.1.4).

transactions carried out with a specific address.[10] Users are therefore advised to use their addresses only once and to generate a new address for each new transaction [52].

Each user-address has its own set of values.[11] It is also possible to use multiple wallets for different purposes. These generally contain the following information:

- a cryptographic key pair (or also several),
- an address generated using the key pair,
- a list of transactions carried out by and addressed to the user,
- other functionalities that depend on the provider of the software.

It is important, above all, that the users sufficiently protect their private key. Because the one who has the private key is allowed to trade with the values bound to it, more specifically to the P2PKH address (further information in Sect. 4.1.1).

3.2 Exchange Among Equals

One of the key strengths of blockchain technology is its architecture. It makes available to multiple users a decentralized, autonomous and secure system.

In the following, we introduce the decentralized system behind blockchain technology. We explain how the information, for example, in the form of transactions traded values such as bitcoins, can reach their new owner.

A blockchain-based system is built on a so-called peer-to-peer network (P2P).[12] The peers are the system users. These, or more precisely their user apps (in the following referred to only as users), represent the nodes in the network. They all have equal rights and can use services and make them available to other users. In the case of the Bitcoin system, it is Bitcoin users who have the Bitcoin app on their computer. With the help of this app they can use the Bitcoin service and the Bitcoin infrastructure to transfer bitcoins or to receive them. At the same time, they are a part of the Bitcoin infrastructure, as they save the complete blockchain,[13] verify it, disseminate the received data, and update the blockchain. In the area of the Internet

---

[10]This expresses the original idea of a blockchain system as a secure, decentralized register.

[11]These values can only be traded if the user has the corresponding private key(s) that match(es) the user address.

[12]A P2P network – peer-to-peer network – is a computer network in which all computers work together on an equal basis. This means that each computer can offer other computers functions and services and, on the other hand, may use functions, resources, services, and files offered by the other computers. The data is distributed across many computers. The P2P concept is a decentralized concept, without a centralized server. Each computer in such a network can be connected with several other computers [144].

[13]The term blockchain here refers to all of the transactions that have ever been carried out in the respective system. This affects the public blockchain and the consortium blockchain (see Sect. 4.1.4).

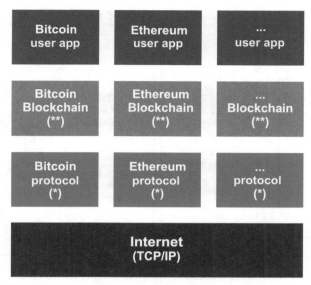

* - Consensus algorithm, assigned value, set of rules
** - Architecture: transactions, blocks, chain, P2P

Fig. 3.4   Abstract representation of the blockchain layer architecture

of Things (IoT) the nodes are, however, IoT devices or IoT gateways that interact with each other in the decentralized network.

In P2P networks, communication takes place via an unencrypted Internet connection (see Fig. 3.4).

Because P2P networks have no authentication mechanisms nor a central administration point for users, the usual methods implemented by P2P networks for finding other nodes and for disseminating information are carried out (see Fig. 3.5) [4].

Basically, in a blockchain system[14] all nodes are "created equal" and can be both clients (service users) and servers (service providers). If we look at the size of the Bitcoin Blockchain (in May 2020: 277 GB), it is understandable that not every user is able to have enough resources for storage and verification. The application should be as "lean" as possible, especially for mobile users. Thus in a blockchain system there are two types of users [4]:

- "Servers," or `full nodes` have both incoming and outgoing connections to other users. This means that they "ask" other users for a connection using their

---

[14] Applies to the public blockchain and the consortium blockchain (see Sect. 4.1.4).

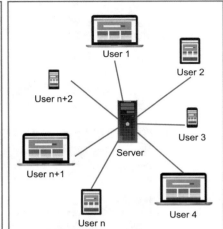

Fig. 3.5 Comparison of P2P and client-server networks

IP addresses, or they are asked by other users for a connection. The full users save the entire blockchain[15] and are involved in the verification process.

- "Clients," or `lightweight nodes` (light nodes, thin clients or, more rarely, SPV[16] nodes) are the most common[17] users in blockchain-based systems. These only have outgoing connections and only save a part of the blockchain [13]. They set up a connection to full nodes to get information that only affects them. Additionally, users who have a different IP address externally as, for example, inside their company network[18] are among the clients.

Both types of users (client and server) in the Bitcoin system support eight outgoing connections to other users. A full Bitcoin node supports additionally up to 117 incoming connections. This division makes sense both for reasons of security[19] as well as for reasons of scalability.[20] We find the same division, only with other numbers, in other blockchain-based systems, such as e.g., Ethereum.

---

[15]Here the term blockchain is understood to include all of the resources associated with it, including the database. In the Bitcoin system these are, for example, all transactions that have ever been executed.

[16]SPV – Simplified Payment Verification (see Sects. 4.2.2 and 5.1.3).

[17]It is estimated that there are 13 times as many clients as servers in the Bitcoin system [4].

[18]For example, users behind a firewall or NAT.

[19]An attacker node is not able to manipulate more than eight other nodes at the same time.

[20]The number of lightweight nodes is much higher. That means that the full nodes, which are already in the minority, must have more incoming connections.

If one of the outgoing connection is no longer active (e.g., because the user is offline), this connection is replaced by a new one [4]. Information is exchanged via this connection, e.g. new transactions, blocks, or IP addresses[21] of the full nodes (servers). Every user (client and server) maintains a list of multiple IP addresses of other full nodes (servers) in the network and updates them regularly by exchanging them with other users. The IP addresses are not linked to the cryptographic addresses.

Back to the example of Alice and Bob. Alice is often on the go and wants to be able to use the Bitcoin system on her laptop. Let's assume that her laptop doesn't have enough memory and computing capacity to run a full node. We will also take into account that she always logs into different networks: at home, in the library, or at the office. She installs the Bitcoin software and sets up a lightweight wallet. The software already contains pre-programmed DNS names[22] (also known as DNS seeds, e.g., seed.bitcoin.sipa.be, seed-.bitcoinstats.com etc.), that contain several IP addresses of full nodes (see Fig. 3.6).

The software then establishes connections with some of the full nodes from the list and asks them for further IP addresses. The list of IP addresses is constantly updated. Thus, the software from Alice can support up to eight connections. This means, that Alice can exchange information with eight other users – in this case full nodes. First, the "lean" version of the current blockchain is downloaded. Alice also sends her transactions to the nodes and receives from them the information that is only intended for her. The disadvantage of a lightweight node is its lower level of security. Alice must trust the full node because she is only using the "lean" version of the blockchain and therefore cannot check all of the previous transactions.

[22]The Domain Name System (DNS) combines numeric (IPv4) and alphanumeric (IPv6) IP addresses with easy to remember domain names so that users are not forced to remember number sequences, but instead meaningful names. For example, hiding behind the DNS name hpi.de is the IPv4 address 141.89.225.126.

The information in a blockchain-based system is exchanged according to fixed rules. These prevent, for example, that information which is already sent by one user (e.g., block, transaction or IP address) can be sent twice to another user. In this way, the network is also protected from overload.

---

[21]In the Bitcoin network: IPv4, IPv6, and OnionCat addresses [4, 13].

Fig. 3.6 Resolution of the
domain name of a DNS seed

```
Name:      seed.bitcoin.sipa.be
Addresses:  2600:1f14:34a:fe00:9ee5:a8f6:6b2a:866e
           2001:470:27:79::2
           2001:470:1f15:106:fa05:465b:f1cd:c83f
           2a01:e0a:cc:add0:8c7c:e48b:210e:4089
           2001:470:6c80:101::1
           2001:67c:2db8:6::44
           2001:67c:2db8:6::45
           2a01:4f8:192:4a4::2
           2001:818:e245:f800:4df:2bdf:ecf5:eb60
           2001:8d8:939:1900::77:9e09
           2001:985:55a0:1::2
           2001:bc8:32d7:1bf:0:242:ac11:4
           2001:bc8:3bec:100::1
           2001:bc8:4700:2000::231b
           2001:19f0:5:35ed:5400:2ff:fe98:a318
           3.133.125.238
           74.83.193.4
           192.129.186.62
           18.237.223.114
           91.106.188.229
           51.154.71.149
           24.34.61.18
           47.75.100.150
           190.189.140.13
           107.178.98.66
           83.51.251.166
           159.100.248.234
           91.222.128.59
           178.248.200.126
           47.90.89.94
           188.214.128.18
           3.15.34.184
           18.141.160.175
           104.248.139.211
           104.248.40.142
           2.224.246.80
           185.175.46.207
           118.163.120.179
           73.7.135.222
           185.21.223.231
```

In contrast to the example of Alice, let us assume that Bob runs a full node. He then has a complete copy of the blockchain and, besides the eight outgoing connection to other users, can have up to 117 incoming connections. Via these connections, he receives all new transactions and blocks of the other users, verifies them according to defined rules, and forwards them. The valid information (e.g., blocks or transactions) are stored in the user's cache (memory pool or "mempool"), the invalid information is discarded.

Fig. 3.7 Dissemination of
information in a
blockchain-based network

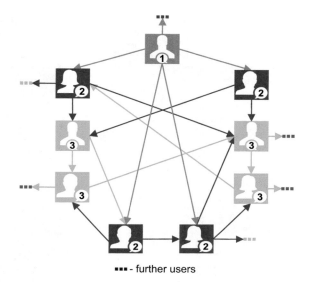

■■■ - further users

The full nodes are the backbone of the Bitcoin system. They allow the system to grow and at the same time remain secure and decentralized.

All information (new blocks, transactions and IP addresses) is passed from one user to another (Fig. 3.7). The full nodes pass on some new transactions together with the newly received ones, so that it appears to the other users as if it were their own.

A node checks the information received according to the defined rules each time. If he has already received the same data/information from another user (i.e., it has already been saved in his memory pool), he discards the newly arrived data.

3.2.1 Obfuscation

As already mentioned, transparency is one of the most essential properties of blockchain technology. In many application areas, however, this property would restrict or violate the privacy of the user. But if the focus is, for example, on the traceability of different ingredients[23] in food or the traceability of information about the storage status[24] (temperature and humidity) of a drug along the supply chain,

---

[23]The ClearKarma company offers a solution for continuous traceability of the ingredients used in the food industry [92]. The company plans a cloud-based platform with detailed information about food products, with the history of all information changes verified and stored in the blockchain.

[24]The Modum.io company offers a solution for continuous data integrity in a supply chain using blockchain technology [157].

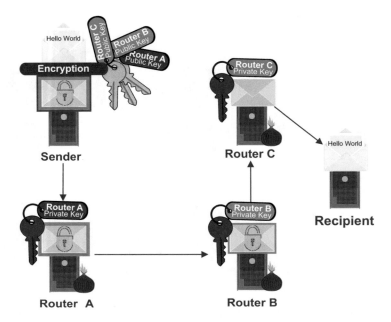

Fig. 3.8 TOR network

transparency and forgery protection are of central importance. In matters of private finances, on the other hand, this is usually not desired.

It should be noted that the anonymity of users, enabled through the use of pseudonyms, is only partially effective, as IP addresses and transaction history make it possible to find out a user's identity (see Sects. 3.1.2 and 4.2).

Bitcoin therefore recommends that its users (lightweight nodes) use the anonymous network TOR in order to disguise (obfuscate) their IP addresses [52]. With the standard software Bitcoin Core[25] full nodes can automatically use the "TOR Hidden Services" for greater anonymity (see Appendix B) [65].

The TOR network provides a service that anonymizes the connection data. The name TOR is an abbreviation that stands for "The Onion Routing." As the name implies, so-called onion routing is characterized by the multiple encryption of a message. The TOR client thereby, searches for a route through the network, which consists of a number of onion servers (onion routers) each of whom provides a public key (Fig. 3.8).

As a rule, the route passes though three servers. After a route has been found, the TOR client first encrypts the message with the public key of the last onion server (router C) and then adds its address. Afterwards, the already encrypted message and

---

[25]Since Version 0.12.0, was published on 23 February 2016.

the address of router C are encrypted with the public key of the second to last server (router B) and its address is added, etc.

After that, the message is decrypted layer by layer during transmission by multiple onion servers. Each server involved in the routing is able to decrypt the message intended for it with its own private key. In turn, within the message it finds a further encrypted message and another address. The message is then forwarded ("not understood") to the given address. In this way, every onion server only "knows" its predecessor and its successor. Only the last link in the routing chain is able to decrypt the actual message and read it in plain text.

The implementation of a TOR network is only possible for outgoing connections. To support incoming connections in the TOR network, the user can make use of the so-called hidden services.[26] In this case, the full node acts as a service provider and arranges a "meeting point" with the service recipient (another user). This is a secure onion server, also known as a rendezvous point. This is done as a means of ensuring secure and anonymous communication [65].

Since there are no sender addresses in the Bitcoin system,[27] it is expressly recommended that to protect its private sphere the user make use of a new address each time a payment is received. To further conceal the recipient, the previously mentioned mixing service can also be used. The legality of using such services may be subject to different rules depending on the laws of the country involved [52].

The listed methods offer more anonymity in the otherwise transparent blockchain system. Nevertheless, users should take increased safety precautions to protect their privacy, as well as to protect the blockchain values (cryptocurrency such as bitcoins; possession of something such as a rented bike; or as an authorization to unlock the door of a room).

3.2.2 Data Protection and Liability

As we have seen, a blockchain-based system has no central authority (it functions in a decentralized and autonomous manner and with a high level of transparency) [52]. These characteristics, which at first glance appear very positive, also lead to data protection issues.

The transparency of all data allows the business and, subsequently in principle, also the personal relationships of users to be recognizable [29]. Trust-critical transactions are exchanged between parties without the necessity of disclosing the identity of the contractual partners to each other or to the public. In this way, anonymity or pseudonymity are employed as data protection instruments [102].

---

[26]TOR hidden services.

[27]Simply put, each transaction contains the Bitcoin value and the recipient address and is then signed by the sender. The user can only issue the received Bitcoin value with its private key, which it has created together with the public key for the transaction (see Sect. 4.1.1).

According to Pesch and Böhme [29] bitcoins (and cryptocurrency in general) can neither be unequivocally classified as the legal object "item" nor the legal object "money." For this reason, because of the prohibition in criminal law of analogies[28] that incriminate the perpetrator, bitcoins (and cryptocurrency in general) cannot be the object of criminal offenses whose facts only relate to item or money [29]. It remains to be seen whether other blockchain values can be described as "item."

One of the most widespread application areas of blockchain technology is the smart contract.[29] The smart contract impacts areas of life that have traditionally been regulated by analog law or institutions [102]. The company Agrello [42] has taken up this problem and presents a solution in the form of legally binding smart contracts. Agrello offers a product with a user-friendly interface that supports the user in the creation of a legally binding contract. The created contract is transformed into an smart contract and stored in a blockchain. At the same time, a legally binding contract in natural language is drawn up and digitally signed [42]. The user is supported during the creation of the contract by an AI[30] agent.

3.3 Consensus Finding

In previous chapters, we have already described several challenges facing decentralized systems when compared to centralized models. Processes such as user authentication, and resource and system administration are distributed to all users in the system. The biggest challenge thereby is to reach an agreement on a state of the system that is "true for everybody" – in other words, which order and execution of content is correct and which is not. This agreement, or "consensus," can, for example, be made difficult by incorrect information from malicious users.

The problem of consensus finding is also known as the "Byzantine Generals Problem." The name comes from a scientific work by Leslie Lamport, Robert Shostak and Marshall Pease [19] and describes an allegory[31] of the consensus finding problem in a decentralized network. The components of a computer system are compared with a group of Byzantine generals.[32] The generals communicate through a messenger and must agree on a common strategy. Both the generals and the messengers could be traitors and try to manipulate loyal communication partners

---

[28]"The prohibition of analogy exists particularly in criminal law. Accordingly, a judge is forbidden from convicting someone of a non-punishable act, even if the judge deems it to be punishable, or if it bears resemblance to another act that is punishable but it does not fully comply with it. This ban applies above all to loopholes in the law." – Definition according to [146].

[29]For further information see Sect. 5.1.2.

[30]AI – Artificial Intelligence.

[31]Rational comprehensible image as representation of an abstract term [104].

[32]During the siege of Constantinople in 1453 AD, the Byzantine generals were to attack the city with their troops.

in decision making. The solution to the problem is an algorithm that helps the loyal generals to reach an agreement in spite of the traitors.

The more malicious users a decentralized system can tolerate under real conditions,[33] the more robust the solution must be. In Castro and Liskov's solution [7] "Practical Byzantine Fault Tolerance (PBFT)," for example, up to a third of malicious users (also called Byzantine faults) are tolerated. The biggest weakness of this solution is its scalability. The more participants (users) the system has, the more messages must be exchanged within the framework of the consensus between participants. In this way, the runtime increases quadratically with the number of system users.

In the past, consensus solutions for decentralized systems were dependent on numerous conditions (permissioned system). For instance, the number of system users and/or their identities had to be generally known. With decentralized networks such as the Internet (permissionless system), this would, however, be highly inefficient if not impossible. In contrast, the Nakamoto consensus mechanism anchored in blockchain technology and used for the first time in the Bitcoin system also works in networks without any conditions for the number of system users or their identification (permissionless system). Users are free to join and leave the network at will [24].

The Nakamoto consensus solution makes the assumption that in a system without participation conditions (malicious users can create many false identities) the majority of the computing power is in the hands of honest users and not that the majority of users are honest. This ensures the robustness of blockchain technology [28].

But what does this have to do with computing power? Instead of selecting master users (master nodes) who make a majority decision by coordinating with other users, any user who solves a computational task faster than any other system user, is allowed to make the decision. This concept is known as Proof-of-Work (PoW). The computational task consists of simply trying out any number of hash values to find a value that corresponds to the target. To do this as quickly as possible, a user needs highly efficient hardware that can, for example,[34] calculate/attempt 15 million hashes in a second. This hardware, therefore, has a much higher energy consumption than what is usual. For the attacker, this is an equally high energy consumption and accordingly means much higher costs (see Sect. 4.1.3 and 51 percent attack in Sect. 4.2). The "winner" can expect a reward, intended as a motivation to put forth computing effort. Because in the Bitcoin system the reward partly consists of newly minted bitcoins, which are distributed to the creator of the new block, the process is compared with that of extracting raw materials, and one speaks of mining.

---

[33]For example, in the Internet. Such solutions as the Byzantine Agreement (BA) Algorithm (see Appendix A) Paxos or Raft are intended for decentralized systems with limited/static users numbers. A majority decision is made between the pre-selected users (so-called master users or master nodes).

[34]NVIDIA GeForce GTX 1050 Ti with the Ethereum algorithm [156].

Correspondingly, a user who creates new blocks is called a miner: "whoever mines carries out hard work to get to the desired material."

The consensus solutions are implemented by algorithms, which are implemented in the form of protocols.[35] What exactly is the reason for an agreement and what decision are the users of a blockchain-based system allowed to make regarding the use of their computing capacity? We have previously written that users have to agree on a state of the system that is "true for everybody." Since all resources are distributed to all users in the system, this means that everyone has an identical copy of all data in the system (replicated database), its order (time stamp) and the execution of content is expected to be correct (i.e., not manipulated). Every user thus checks the information received from other users (e.g. IP addresses of other users, transactions, and blocks) and saves this in his cache (memory pool).

At this point, decision-making comes into play – namely which received information and in which order is written into the system (database). Because the information (data) takes different times to be spread in the network due to the network delays, different users can have different copies of the system (database). The order, or more precisely the time stamp, is implemented in a blockchain-based system using hash chains.

The information (data) already included in the cache (memory pool) is put into hash chain form by those users competing for the reward. First, the information[36] is compiled in a compact form of limited size[37] called a block (more on this subject in Sect. 4.1.2). The block should be linked with the information already available in the system, namely with the already existing blocks. For this, we create a block header with a reference to the last block in the system. This reference is nothing more than a hash of the block header of the previous block. After a block has been prepared (more on this in Sects. 4.1.1, 4.1.2 and 4.1.3) and the computing task has been solved, the block, together with the solution, is distributed to all users in the same way as the other data in the system (information: IP addresses of other users, transactions). Each user receives the new block, verifies it and adds it to the previous block (last block). Thus an ordered blockchain is created.

If several users solve the computational task at the same time, this causes the chain to branch – creating a so-called fork. The probability that more than two users arrive at a solution at the same time is very low. This means that two new blocks have the same previous block and are distributed with different delays in the network. This results in users having different blockchains (copies of the system). Other reward-motivated users link their new block to the block they received first. The longest chain is always given preference because it is not worthwhile for users to continue to "build" a chain that will ultimately not prevail. This economically-motivated decision represents the consensus. Through the linking of the new block

---

[35] Definition of standards and conventions for a smooth data transmission between computers [104].

[36] In the Bitcoin system, e.g., in the form of transactions transferred values – bitcoins.

[37] In the Bitcoin system, for example, 1 MB and in Ethereum approx. 27 kB (as of May 2020).

with one of the branched preceding blocks, the user votes for one of the two chains in the form of computing capacity. This means that the chain with the most votes (in other words, with the greatest computing capacity) "wins." In this way, the decentralized system remains "consistent."

The competition for the reward in the Bitcoin system has led to an "upgrade" of hardware among users (miners) involved in consensus building. Many miners combine to form so-called mining pools so as to bundle their computing capacity. This has led to a constant increase in energy consumption and of the costs associated with it. The charge of energy waste is the greatest point of contention in the Proof-of-Work concept.

In contrast, the consensus concept called Proof-of-Stake (PoS) is not based on the effort expended in solving a computational task, but on the proportion of digital coins in a cryptocurrency. A user who have the n percent of the digital coins, may create n percent of the blocks.

In the Peercoin system[38] (uses PoS and PoW – hybrid consensus) the usable portion of digital coins is based on the "age of the coins." The number of digital coins that a block producer owns is multiplied by the number of days in which the digital coins are kept at the block producer (e.g., if Alice has received 5 coins from Bob and these have already been kept in her blockchain application (wallet) for 10 days, the coin age is thus 50 coin days). For successful block generation, the coin age must be between 30 and 90 days. The block producer addresses these digital coins in the first transaction to himself when the block is created. After that, they are first valid for minting (block generation in PoS systems) again in 30 coin days. Every user of the peercoin system can create a block and annually receive a reward worth a maximum of one percent of the digital coins held. The reward consists of newly minted peercoins.

In contrast to the Peercoin and Bitcoin systems, with the cryptocurrency NXT all digital coins are available from the start (Genesis block). Here, the transaction fees serve as motivation for the block creators. NXT uses a modified PoS algorithm [5].

With the pure PoS concept, a problem exists called "nothing at stake." In the event that the chain branches, minters (block generators in PoS) can build new blocks in parallel on both branches without significant losses. In this way, the possibility exists of the "double spending" of digital cryptocoins (double spending problem). Since in this case loss is not as noticeable, as for example with the PoW concept (already consumed energy), the motivation for attackers is greater with PoS, making it more of a vulnerable target [5].

This problem is solved in an expanded form by PoS known as a "delegated Proof-of-Stake." Delegates ("trusted persons," who are users) are selected according to specific criteria (e.g., based on the number of digital coins in their possession or the votes cast by other users). They may participate in minting and verify the blocks created by other delegates. For a new block to be accepted, several delegates must

---

[38]Peercoin is a peer-to-peer cryptocurrency that is based on the design of Satoshi Nakamotos Bitcoin [18].

sign it, following successful verification. In order to avoid attacks, the digital coins of the delegates are blocked in the event of malicious behavior.

A further alternative to PoW and PoS is the Proof-of-Burn concept (PoB). Here, digital coins are destroyed during mining (figuratively-speaking "burned"). The more digital coins are destroyed, the higher the chance that the newly created block will be accepted and entered into the chain. The digital cryptocoins to be destroyed are sent to an address where they can no longer be used.

Within the Stellar Consensus Protocol (SCP), work continues to be carried out on solving the problem of the Byzantine generals.[39] Stellar is a public finance platform that makes it easy to send money in different currencies. SCP is based on a new consensus model that was described for the first time in the SCP white paper.[40] It is called the Federated Byzantine Agreement (FBA). In the FBA, users do not need a full overview of all other users in the system. Every user has a free choice of trusted membership groups – so-called quorum slices. A quorum is a quantity of users necessary to reach an agreement. A quorum slice is the subset of a quorum that can convince a particular user of the agreement. Each user can have multiple slices that can be chosen based on their reputation or the respective financial arrangement [23].

The quorums can overlap if they have common users. In order to reach an agreement, the FBA users coordinate with each other. To facilitate this they use so-called federated voting. Because of the overlap of quorums, the slices can mutually influence each other in decision making. New digital coins in the Stellar system, also known as Lumens (XLM), are awarded weekly to users through such a vote (one percent annual creation rate).

In decentralized networks, the consistent distribution of resources is an essential property. This is guaranteed in Blockchain-based systems by a user's vote for the longest chain. Since malicious users can manipulate voting (double spending, Sybil attack), various mechanisms are used to regulate voting. As part of the Proof-of-Work concept, votes are cast in the form of physical resources (energy consumption through an outlay of computing power). In order to keep losses as low as possible and to win the competition for the reward, users must abide by the rules (build correct blocks). The expensive alternative is to convince other nodes of the correctness of the blocks by means of the highest computing power (more than 51 percent).

Under these circumstances, the "penalty" for malicious behavior is relatively high. This is an even greater motivation for individual miners (block creators who are not involved in any mining pools) to act according to the rules defined in the system. The probability is very low that in a system with many users, such as

---

[39]Byzantine Agreement (BA, see Appendix A).
[40]White Paper of 25 February 2016.

Bitcoin, one of them has more computing power than all other nodes put together (over 51 percent of the total computing power[41]).

Concepts such as PoS and PoB solve the problem of the wasteful use of energy by shifting the focus from the physical to the electronic resources. Yet at the same time, this increases the likelihood of a branching of the chain and of double spending, which in turn can be resolved with further restrictions (e.g., with the delegated Proof-of-Stake concept).

---

[41] There is indeed also the possibility to launch an attack with less computing capacity than 50 percent of the entire network. The success rate is, however, correspondingly low (see Sect. 4.2).

Chapter 4
Where Does the Hype End, and Where Does the Innovation of Blockchain Technology Begin?

Abstract Now we are ready to go deeper into the subject matter, and you have a chance to form a first opinion about blockchain technology – is it an innovation or only hype? Thereby, we will take a closer look at the architecture of blockchain technology using well-known examples such as Bitcoin and Ethereum and addressing challenges including security and scalability.

Although blockchain technology is still relatively young, it has become a much talked about topic of conversation everywhere. The enigmatic Bitcoin project as the first implementation of the technology, and its rapid dissemination in many different areas, has initially turned the topic of blockchain into one surrounded by hype. Time and again, the media reports on new, unbelievable increases or sharp drops in value, and even about the possible demise of the bitcoin.

In its Hype Cycle for Emerging Technologies 2016 [36], Gartner, the word's leading research and advisory company, placed blockchain in the Peak of Inflated Expectations (see Fig. 4.1). In this phase, "early publicity produces a number of success stories – often accompanied by scores of failures. Some companies take action; many do not." [123]

After the initial interest of the media faded – we believe this is likely due to the fact that the technology still finds itself in its infancy, regarding elaborated cross-technology standards, uniform interfaces and proven cases of application – technology moved to the next phase of the Hype Cycle. According to Gartner's Hype Cycle for Emerging Technologies 2017 [37], blockchain experienced a descent into the Trough of Disillusionment.

Specific standards and uniform interfaces will likely be set after the new technology overcomes its expected decline and the unfulfilled expectations and negative reports that accompany it. We believe this will lead to the next phase, the Slope of Enlightenment, from which the Plateau of Productivity will then be reached. Realized in this phase will also be a greater application on the market. As long as blockchain technology lacks mature and uniform standards, it will hang in the balance between the hype of unrealistic expectations and its place as an innovation whose solutions are still marked by random difficulties.

© Springer Nature Switzerland AG 2021
T. Gayvoronskaya, C. Meinel, *Blockchain*,
https://doi.org/10.1007/978-3-030-61559-8_4

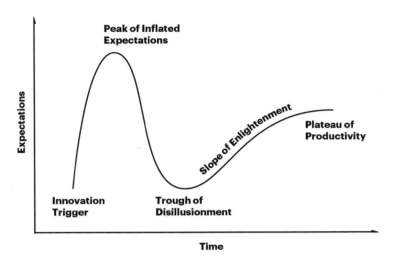

Fig. 4.1 Generic Gartner Hype Cycle Graphic (2020) [123]

In the previous chapters, we already revealed part of the blockchain hype and showed that, as opposed to being a cure-all, blockchain technology is in reality a successful combination of existing technological approaches from the areas of cryptography, decentralized networks and consensus-finding models. In this chapter, we would like to explore the real strengths and challenges of blockchain technology and provide a technical overview.

4.1   Traceability, Forgery Protection, Reliability

The use of a new technology in an existing system must offer specific advantages, for instance an increase in efficiency or a reduction in costs. This is the same with the use of blockchain technology. Particular attention must be paid to those properties in the technology that bring added benefits, when compared to already established technical solutions. Thereby, attention is focused on the original idea of a blockchain: namely of providing a secure decentralized public register.

The traceability of all entries in the system and the associated security against forgery make blockchain technology particularly attractive for logging data. For example, it offers a basis for various registers, such as a land or a medical register. Additionally, blockchain technology allows a secure, decentralized and transparent exchange of values between the numerous involved users – without the need for a trusted middleman (also called a trusted third party). This means that the data to be recorded (e.g., possession of a value) can be written into the blockchain by multiple

Fig. 4.2 Blockstack-layer
architecture

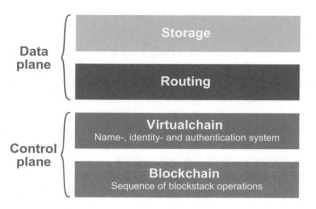

parties and can also be read from the blockchain. The distribution[1] of the blockchain
on any number of independent computers provides protection in the event of system
failure or data loss.

In regards to data protection, only cryptographic fingerprints of the data (hash
values) can be stored in the blockchain in a tamper-proof manner, for example. The
actual data can be stored elsewhere.[2]

For example, the Blockstack identity system uses the advantages of blockchain
technology and only records the Blockstack operations in the blockchain (Fig. 4.2).
The other functionalities, such as the management and storage of data, are regulated
outside of the blockchain (for more information see Sect. 6.2).

In contrast, pure cryptocurrencies have a simpler architecture (see Fig. 3.4):

- Blockchain as the foundation,
- Specific rules for the respective cryptocurrency (among them the consensus
  algorithm) and
- A user application in which everything is implemented.

Based on these issues, the individual blockchain applications differ from each
other. Some of them are clearly more complex in their structure than others. However, what they all have in common is their underlying architecture (a cryptographic
timestamp service/a cryptographic linking of the blocks and a consensus represented
by the longest chain – see Sect. 3.3).

Only when blockchain architecture is fully understood, do properties such as
protection against forgery and traceability become completely clear. In the following
chapters we would like to take as starting point the content/information that is
included in the decentralized blockchain database.

---

[1]Replication.

[2]CloudRAID, for instance, provides a suitable infrastructure to do this.

4.1.1 The Smallest Component in a Blockchain

A network based on blockchain technology is often called an `Internet of value`. This term applies to only one of the application areas or, more precisely, the first generation[3] of blockchain-based projects (bitcoin-like projects). A cryptocurrency unit (digital crypto coin), an event or a product[4] – for example, an object offered for sale on a trading platform – can represent a value. In blockchain technology a value always has an owner. The current status of who owns the value is documented in the blockchain register. Consequently, blockchain technology is often compared to a public register.

Behind the second generation of blockchain-based projects is a further development of the original concept of blockchain technology. Not only is a robust and secure decentralized system for logging the ownership of a value possible, but the system acts as a large decentralized computer with millions of autonomous objects (smart contracts), which are able to maintain an internal database, execute code and engage in mutual communication [130]. Ethereum, for example, is among the first projects of the second generation since 2014.

Blockchain projects of both generations are concerned with updating and logging the respective, current state of the system.[5] The first generation deals with the current state of a value; specifically, who owns a certain value (unspent transaction output – UTXO). Blockchain 2.0 deals with the current state of an `Account` (account state – balance, code, internal storage). These accounts are, for example, divided into two types in an Ethereum network: external and internal accounts. External accounts[6] are comparable to a bank account and have an "account number," more specifically an address,[7] and information about the balance and transactions that have been made via the address. Users of the Ethereum system have external accounts, and can by means of transactions "transfer" Ether[8] to other external accounts or activate internal accounts – that are assigned to the autonomous objects (so-called smart contracts). The smart contracts have an address and thus an account and their own code, by which they are controlled (for more on the subject of smart contracts see Sect. 5.1.2). The code can implement any rules and conditions

---

[3]The use of blockchain technology is not only limited to the areas of cryptocurrency or decentralized registers, but the technology is used as a programmable decentralized trust infrastructure [192], the so-called Blockchain 2.0 (smart contracts).

[4]Based on the supply-oriented definition, a product is everything that is offered on the market for use or consumption and that satisfies a wish or a need. Accordingly, not only physical objects are referred to as products, but also various services, ideas, etc. fall under the category of products. This term encompasses all materials and immaterial facets from which customer benefits can result [40, 163].

[5]Therefore blockchain technology is often called a "replicated state machine."

[6]Externally owned account – EOA.

[7]Similar to a Bitcoin address – see Sect. 3.1.2.

[8]The digital cryptocurrency of the Ethereum system.

and thus allow complex applications. These applications run without any central "coordinator" on computers of all full nodes and accordingly form a censorship-resistant, decentralized world computer [38, 74, 130].

The current state of a value or an account is updated using a transaction. In this way, the transaction represents a bridge, or valid transition between two states – the previous one and the current one [38]. The transaction format and components differ depending on the system. Generally-speaking, a transaction consists of specific data, values, or code (transaction for the creating a smart contract), of one or more recipient addresses, parameters that are typical for the particular system, and the digital signature of the sender.

Blockchain projects of the first generation only log the current state of a value and have a relatively simple transaction structure. This structure has two essential components: an input and an output. The value to be transferred (which the user already has) is referenced in the input. The output indicates to which address this value is to be "overwritten." In other words, an output of the already valid transaction is referenced through which the sender received the value at an earlier point in time. In the case of a cryptocurrency, an input can contain multiple crypto coins, thus in the output must indicate the number of crypto coins from the given input and the address to which they are to be issued.

A newly created value, for instance a newly minted digital crypto coin or a new object for sale on a trading platform, has no prior history. In this case, the transaction input is empty. The output in this case represents the object or a number of newly minted crypto coins and indicates the recipient's address (the owner of this value), for example the hash value of the public key of the block creator (miner). Only with the next transaction, when the value is "overwritten" from one user to another, will the previous output (unspent transaction output – UTXO) be referenced in the input. This reference to an UTXO consists of a hash value of the transaction that contains this output as well as an output index, since a transaction can contain multiple outputs.

In the Bitcoin system, all previous transactions that have been addressed to a user, but not yet been issued, are listed in the user's wallet as the current Bitcoin holdings. These previous transactions are used in new transactions of this user as inputs. Several outputs are possible if the value to be transferred is divided between several recipients. If the sender wishes to transfer a smaller amount of money than that which is available through all inputs put together, the sender has the option of transferring the remaining amount to himself. If the sender has a leftover amount in his transaction that he does not transfer back to himself, it is then considered a transaction fee (Fig. 4.3). Transactions cannot be reversed.

In the Bitcoin system, the output is locked by a mechanism called ScriptPubKey [44]. ScriptPubKey consists of a series of instructions that describe how the owner of the respective recipient address can gain access to the value [66]. In addition to the reference to the value, another mechanism is required in the input. This is ScriptSig. It unlocks the value, after the conditions set in the previous output are

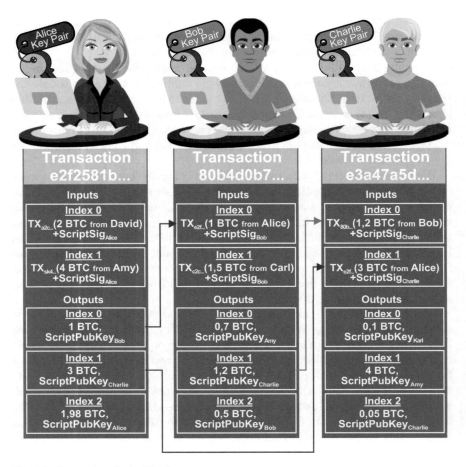

Fig. 4.3 Transactions in the Bitcoin system

fulfilled, for example if the sender can prove a suitable address and a signature that corresponds to the address (Fig. 4.4).[9]

In 2012, in the context of the BIP16,[10] in the Bitcoin system, a new functionality was implemented. It gives Bitcoin recipients a way to define instructions about how the received bitcoins can be issued later, or, more specifically, how they can be unlocked. Thus a so-called Pay-to-Script hash address (P2SH address) is defined.

---

[9] As previously described, the address corresponds to the hash of the public key. In this way, the sender can use the values (or more specifically, the UTXOs) addressed to him only if, in addition to the public key, he has a matching secret key (private key), which he uses for signing.

[10] Bitcoin Improvement Proposal (BIP) is a design document for the introduction of functions or information in Bitcoin [56].

```
Input:
Previous tx: f5d8ee39a430901c91a5917b9f2dc19d6d1a0e9cea205b009ca73dd04470b9a6
Index: 0
scriptSig: 304502206e21798a42fae0e854281abd38bacd1aeed3ee3738d9e1446618c4571d10
90db022100e2ac980643b0b82c0e88ffdfec6b64e3e6ba35e7ba5fdd7d5d6cc8d25c6b241501

Output:
Value: 5000000000
scriptPubKey: OP_DUP OP_HASH160 404371705fa9bd789a2fcd52d2c580b65d35549d
OP_EQUALVERIFY OP_CHECKSIG
```

Fig. 4.4 Example of a Bitcoin transaction with an input and an output

This is often used for multi-signature transactions, for example. Just as with the pay-to-public-key hash address (P2PKH address) previously described, a hash value is specified as the address in the output, or more precisely in the ScriptPubKey. Only in the case of P2SH is the hash value from a "script"[11] (a series of instructions) and not just one public key. This means in the next transaction that will "spend" the value, an appropriate unlocking mechanism must be used. In this case, the ScriptSig does not only provide a signature and a matching public key for verification, but a script and the necessary data (public keys and signatures).

The transaction structure in the blockchain projects of the second generation is significantly more complex. In the Ethereum system a distinction is made between two types of transactions: transactions that are "exchanged" between the accounts and transactions that are used to create new smart contracts (contract creation transactions). Transactions that are exchanged between the accounts are in turn again divided into two types: transactions that are made by external accounts, and so-called messages that are exchanged between the internal accounts of the smart contracts. An Ethereum transaction consists of the following:

- Nonce – A value that corresponds to the number of transactions carried out by the sender,
- gasPrice – A fee charged in the Ethereum system for every step of calculation in a smart contract. The fees are imposed for security reasons (protection against denial of service attacks), whereby every user, including attackers, should pay for every resource that is used (including calculation, bandwidth, and storage). The fee is measured in units of gas and paid in Ether – Ethereum's own cryptocurrency. Thus, in every transaction, the current rate of a unit of gas is noted in determining the cost to execute the transaction.
- gasLimit – A value corresponding to the maximum amount of gas that is to be used in executing the transaction. It is paid in advance before any calculation is made and cannot be increased later. gasLimit is used to avoid accidental or intentional endless loops or other calculation problems in the code. For this

---

[11]To be more exact: a hash value acquired from the script and the data necessary for it, such as multiple public keys.

reason, in every transaction a limit is set on the number of calculation steps that can be carried out in the code.

- Recipient address (In the case of a contract creation transaction, this field is empty),
- Value – The amount of Ether that is to be transferred from the sender to the recipient (in the case of a contract creation transaction, the amount of Ether for the newly created smart contract account),
- Data that is used for the signing of the transaction and to determine the sender of the transaction,
- Smart contract code for the contract creation transaction,
- Data for a message (transactions that are exchanged between the smart contracts) [38, 133].

After a transaction has been created, it is passed on to other users with whom a connection exists. Transactions and blocks are distributed from user to user in the system. There is no certain route from one user to another through which the data (transactions, blocks, IP addresses) are transferred, instead every full node verifies the received transaction according to defined rules (see Appendix C), stores a copy in its cache (memory pool) and distributes it to a lot of other users (see Sect. 3.2). Thus, the current state of a value or an account is logged in the blockchain. This also means that every user can keep track of who owned a value and when, and what the state of an account was at a certain time.

Here are four examples used to verify transactions in the Bitcoin system:

- A transaction has been signed,
- A transaction has never been "issued" before,
- I add the transaction to my wallet if it has been addressed to me,
- If the transaction has been added to a valid block, it is deleted from my cache.

A transaction is considered valid (e.g., in the Bitcoin system) if it has been included in a block that already has at least five successor blocks. This number was determined based on the assumption that potential attackers do not have enough computing power – or want to expend it – to recalculate six blocks.

4.1.2   Block and Chain

After transactions have been distributed to the full nodes in the blockchain network, and after being successfully verified and added to the cache, users can summarize them in a specific list with additional information, for which they receive a reward. In blockchain technology, such a list is called a "block." The user only has a chance to create a valid block and receive a reward if the block has been created based on the predefined requirements in his system, and if this block has been included in the longest chain (see Sect. 3.3). In bitcoin-similar projects, Proof-of-Work is necessary in creating a valid block (see Sect. 3.3). In contrast, developers of the Ethereum system are planning to switch from Proof-of-Work to Proof-of-Stake in 2020.

Transactions and blocks are the most important components of a blockchain. Besides containing transactions, blocks include other important information. This information is recorded in the so-called "block header."[12] This information is necessary for the correct construction of the blockchain and its verification.

In the Bitcoin system, a block header contains the following information:

- Nonce[13] – an important indication of the correct building of the block; it is used for mining (32 bit),
- A reference to the previous block: a SHA-256 hash[14] of the previous block header,
- An important value for the building of the block that shows a target[15] for the cryptographic computational task (see Sect. 3.3),
- A block time[16] [50],
- A reference to all transactions in the block, also known as the root of the Merkle tree ("Merkle root," 256 bit),
- The specification of a so-called "block version" (described in the BIP[17] and in one of the Bitcoin core versions[18] introduced block version, which complies with specific features/functions and was introduced as a soft fork[19]).

The hash of the previous block header, the nonce and the difficulty target for the cryptographic computation task are relevant information for mining (creation of a new block) (more of this topic in Sect. 4.1.3).

As shown in the chapter on cryptography, the hash function allows for clear and simple data identification – practical for a fast and unique referencing. In blockchain technology, the hash values help to ensure the correct order of the data/information. They are used as references (the hash value of a transaction or block is the reference to the transaction or block). A transaction contains, for example, the hash values of the previous transactions. These are (e.g., in Bitcoin-like systems) the input values of

---

[12]In the Ethereum system in addition to the block header and the transaction information, a list of other block headers is also provided, so-called "ommers" or in, Ethereum jargon, "uncles" [38].

[13]In cryptography, the term nonce (short for "used only once" or "number used once") is used to describe a number or letter combination that is only used a single time in the respective context [200] (more information in Sect. 4.1.3).

[14]SHA256SHA256(block header).

[15]"Difficulty target": This value is recalculated every two weeks in the Bitcoin system (more on this in Sect. 4.1.3).

[16]More precisely, a time stamp. The block time is a Unix epoch, in which a miner started the creation of the block (of the header to hash – mining).

[17]Bitcoin Improvement Proposal (BIP) is a design document for the introduction of functions or information in Bitcoin [56].

[18]Bitcoin core (formerly known as Bitcoin-Qt) is the third Bitcoin client that was developed by Wladimir van der Laan, based on Satoshi Nakamoto's original reference code [56].

[19]See Sect. 4.1.4.

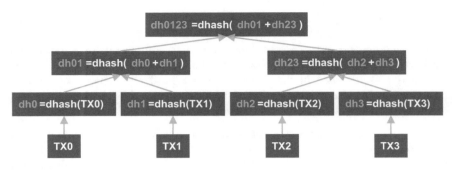

Fig. 4.5 Hash tree consisting of transactions

the transactions (inputs) – specifically, the value holdings/assets (in Bitcoin systems the monetary holdings). In this way, it is possible to track the entire history of the transaction or of the value in the blockchain.

The blocks contain two different references. One refers to the previous block (hash of the block header) and the other refers to all transactions listed in the block. These references are called "fingerprints." The reference to the transactions in the block provides a simple indication of whether a transaction was inserted into the block at a later time or if it has been changed.

The Merkle Root is the last hash value in the so-called hash tree. A hash tree ("Merkle tree") is a tree-like structure (from graph theory) that consists of successive hash values.[20] For example, in Fig. 4.5, we see that in Transaction 1 (**TX1**) a doubled hash value **dh1** is first created. This is **dh1=SHA256(SHA256(TX1))**. The same is done with the transactions **TX0**, **TX2** and **TX3**. Subsequently, further hash values are calculated from the first found doubled hash value of the original transactions. In this case, the root of the tree **dh0123** is the Merkle root.

In contrast to the Bitcoin system, the Ethereum system uses an advanced technology for a cryptographically authenticated data structure, namely the Merkle Patricia Tree.[21] Thus in a Ethereum block header not only is a Merkle Patricia Root of the transaction list (transactionsRoot) saved,[22] but two other roots: one root of the states[23] (stateRoot) and one of the receipts[24] (receiptsRoot). In addition to the three roots, a further twelve entries are stored in an Ethereum block header. For comparison: a Bitcoin block header consists of six entries [38]. This confirms once

---

[20]In the Bitcoin system, the hash function SHA-256 is used twice.

[21]Also called the Merkle Patricia Trie or Patricia Trie. This structure enables a fast search for contents, is easy to implement and needs little storage space [133].

[22]There is a separate transaction tree for each block.

[23]There is a global state tree that is updated over time.

[24]In the Ethereum system a receipt is created for each transaction that contains the specific information regarding its execution (for more on this subject see [38, 133]). Each block has its own receipts tree.

again the higher complexity of the Ethereum system when compared to the Bitcoin system.

In the Bitcoin system, the block size is limited to 1 MB. A block may therefore contain between 900 and 2,500 transactions. The Bitcoin community has long discussed whether the block size should remain at 1 MB or be increased to 2 MB. On August 1, 2017, the new cryptocurrency Bitcoin Cash (BCH) was created by splitting from the Bitcoin system. Here, the size of a block is set at 8 MB. In the Ethereum system, the size of a block is approximately 27 kB (as of May 2020).

One of the requirements for block creation (whether we say "mining" or "minting" depends on the consensus algorithm used, see Sect. 3.3) is that a new block must be created within a certain time. In the Bitcoin system this is 10 minutes (approx. 60 blocks per hour) and with Ethereum a new block is created every 14 seconds (approx. 250 blocks per hour).

In the Bitcoin system, new values (i.e., new bitcoins) are generated when blocks are created. The block creator (miner) creates a new transaction in the process of rewarding himself – a so-called coinbase transaction. This transaction is the first transaction in the block. The input of this transaction is correspondingly empty, as the bitcoins are newly created and as yet have no history. The output is the reward size (number of new bitcoins,[25] in addition to fees that were paid for the transactions included in the block) together with the ScriptPubKey. This transaction is formed into a block with other transactions.[26]

To be sure that the created transaction is valid, users should wait until the transaction has been included in a block, which already contains several successor blocks (at least five in the Bitcoin system).

Because every new block is created within a specified time, the waiting time is correspondingly long. In the Bitcoin system, the waiting time is between one and two hours.

Miners receive the transaction fees for all transactions contained in the block. After a block is created, it is distributed to the users. Each full node verifies the block it has received according to defined rules and adds it to the chain. In this way, a chain is created of successive blocks that are linked together by references. The first block in the chain is also called the genesis block.

Blockchain technology therefore lists all transactions that have ever been carried out in the respective system and included in blocks. The blocks listed form a chain, in which each block contains a reference to the previous one. This results in the creation of an orderly sequence of blocks and is what gave rise to the name "blockchain."

As the blockchain system is decentralized, and between users there is no agreement made as to the priority of the created blocks, it can happen that several

---

[25]Up to 2020 there were 12.5 newly generated bitcoins. After 210,000 blocks, the reward paid to the miner will be halved (approx. every 4 years; for example, starting in 2020 there will be only 6.25 bitcoins).

[26]Transactions of other users that the miner has already stored in its memory pool.

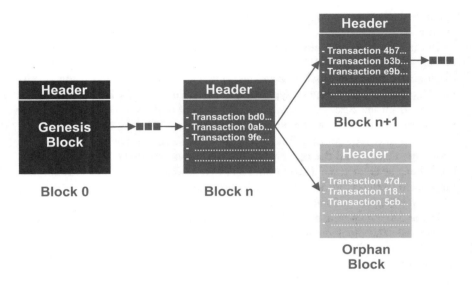

Fig. 4.6 Blockchain

miners create a new block at the same time. If these blocks comply with all the rules
and refer to the last block, the result can be a branching of the chain. This branching
is also called a "fork." The solution for this problem is also the most important
rule in the blockchain system: "The longest chain is valid." (more on this topic in
Sects. 4.1.3 and 3.3). The shortest chain is ignored; its blocks are called "orphan
blocks" (see Fig. 4.6).

The size of the Bitcoin blockchain was approximately 280 GB at the end of May
2020.

4.1.3 Updating the Blockchain

The blockchain is updated by combining new transactions into blocks and cryptographically linking the blocks in a specific order. Because a blockchain-based
system is decentralized, it is necessary that a consensus be reached. One of the
biggest challenges here is to agree upon a state of system that is "right for
everybody." This means in which order the content should be and whether or not
the execution of the content is correct (see Sect. 3.3). Generally-speaking, every full
node can participate in finding a consensus and can update the blockchain. Since
the Nakamoto consensus solution is based on the notion that in a system without

participation requirements[27] the majority of the computing power is in the hands of honest users,[28] full users (full nodes) can cast their vote to reach a consensus in the form of expending computing resources. This is carried out by solving a computational task. The user who solves the computational task faster than all the others in the system is allowed to update the blockchain. This user also gets a reward.[29] This concept is called Proof-of-Work (PoW). The reward in the Bitcoin system therefore serves in the creation and dissemination of new bitcoins. This is also a motivating factor in getting users to participate in the mining process and thus ensuring the security of the system [62].

The computational task consists of simply trying out a random number of hash values to find a value that corresponds to the target. This process is called mining. The users who update the blockchain are called miners. Because, for example, in the Bitcoin system the reward consists in part of newly minted bitcoins, and these are distributed to the creator of the new block, there is indeed a similarity between the mining of raw materials: those who mine must work hard to reach the resources they are after.

Other concepts, such as Proof-of-Stake (PoS) which is not based on the computing effort in solving the computational task but on the proportion of digital coins of a cryptocurrency, are not further pursued in this chapter.

The work expended in mining is deliberately resource-intensive and difficult so that the block creation process remains constant (in the Bitcoin system this means a new block every 10 minutes) and prevents potential attackers from manipulating the blocks or flooding the network with fake blocks. It is likewise necessary for attackers to perform these intensive processes in order to create new blocks.

After the completed transactions have been distributed to all full users, they verify the received transactions and save them in their respective cache (memory pool), until they are included in a block.

Before a miner can include the transactions into a valid block, he has to solve a cryptographic computational task with a certain level of difficulty.[30] The task consists of finding a hash value below the given target ("difficulty target"). The level of difficulty and target are adjusted every two weeks (after 2016 blocks) in such a way that ten minutes are required for the creation of a new block. If the computing power of the entire network increases (or decreases) and the 2016 blocks are found in less (or more) than two weeks, then the level of difficulty is raised or lowered accordingly.

The hash value is determined by the double hash function SHA-256, calculated from the block header and a nonce.[31] The nonce, a 32 bit long, variable hexadecimal

---

[27]Malicious users can generate many false identities.

[28]And not that the majority of users is honest.

[29]In the Bitcoin system the reward consists of newly mined bitcoins and transaction fees.

[30]The level of difficulty indicates how hard it is to find a hash value below the given target.

[31]In cryptography, the term "nonce" is used to denote a combination of numbers or letters that is only used a single time in the respective context [200].

Fig. 4.7 Mining process in solving the cryptographic task

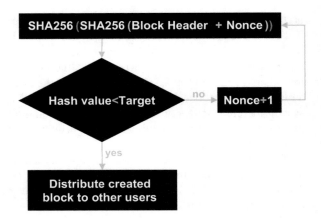

character string, is adjusted continuously until the hash value is less than or equal to the target (see Fig. 4.7).

The target is a 256 bit long hexadecimal string that all full nodes can calculate. The smaller the target (i.e., the more zeros at the beginning of the string), the higher the level of difficulty. If in hash calculation the required number of zeros is generated at the beginning, the task is solved (more on this subject can be found in the [150]).

The likelihood that a user will find the correct solution is proportional to the amount of computing power that he expends (his hash rate[32]). After the appropriate solution is found, the generated block is distributed to all users.

Every full node verifies[33] the received block. Depending on the verification result, the block is accepted (added to the main chain[34] or to the side branch[35]) or discarded (orphan block).[36] If the block is accepted, it will always be sent to the other users (see Sect. 3.2).

Due to the network delay, the blocks spread at different periods of time. When multiple miners solve the computational task at the same time and distribute their blocks simultaneously in the network, after a time only a single chain will finally prevail. Here is an example: Alice and Bob have simultaneously found a solution for the cryptographic computational task and spread their newly created blocks **a** and **b** in the network. After successful verification, each user saves the first received block as part of the main chain (main branch). A user **Dave** receives the block **b** from Bob, after having already received block **a** from Alice. He then adds it to the

---

[32]The hash rate or computing power refers to how many hashing operation can be performed in a second.

[33]First a check is made as to whether the block is structured correctly and whether the references in the block header are correct. For a detailed description of block verification see [64].

[34]Also called the main branch – the longest chain that has been verified by all users as valid.

[35]A side branch is created when a chain branches (fork).

[36]Orphan blocks are either blocks that have no preceding block or the blocks from the shorter chain that were rejected.

side branch after verification and waits for the next block. Charlie is also a miner and received block **b** first. He builds another block **b+1** and distributes it to all users. The user **Dave** receives block **b+1**. After verification, he adds it to his side branch (where Bob's block **b** is stored) and defines it as a main chain, since the longest chain ultimately becomes a main chain. The blocks from the side branch become orphan blocks and their valid transactions are moved again to the user's memory pools. Since the chain with Bob's block has prevailed, Bob gets a reward after a waiting time of 100 blocks. The reward takes the form of newly minted bitcoins and transaction fees. Alice gets no reward for her block **a**.

The number of newly created bitcoins is halved every four years (by 2012 it was 50 BTC, and by July 2016 the number was 25 BTC, by 2020 it was 12.5 BTC, etc.).

In order to solve the computational task with the predetermined level of difficulty as fast as possible, a user needs hardware with an efficient calculating capability, for example,[37] 15 million hashes in a second. In the early years of the Bitcoin system, the level of difficulty of the cryptographic task was considerably lower than now. It was thus possible for Bitcoin users to mine bitcoins with their computer (on the CPU[38] or the GPU).[39] Spurred on by competition for the reward, many Bitcoin users have upgraded their hardware over time (e.g., ASIC[40] mining hardware), which has led to an increase in the computing power of the entire network and also to the level of difficulty of the computational task.

In calculating the computational task, the hardware must expend a considerably higher energy consumption than usual. In December 2017, Bitcoin miners with an energy efficiency of between 0.29 J/GH[41] and 0.098 J/GH and a performance of between 3.5 TH/s[42] and 13.5 TH/s could be found on the market. These consume approx. 1,200 watts. The hash rate[43] of the Bitcoin network was approx. 12,337,091 TH/s [78]. The Bitcoin network thus consumed about 49 GWh in one day. In comparison, an average household in Germany of four people consumes approx. 4,000 kWh of electricity per year. Thus the electricity that the Bitcoin network requires in one day could supply about 12,250 households for one year. The estimation of energy consumption of the Bitcoin network differs widely depending on the source. For example, in September 2017 according to information from Digiconomist the figure was around 19 TWh per year, and in a research paper by Mishra[44] (University of Texas at Dallas) it was 5 GWh. In order to successfully compete today, miners require special hardware and software or must participate in cloud mining. Many miners band together into so-called mining pools to bundle

---

[37]NVIDIA GeForce GTX 1050 Ti with the Ethereum algorithm [156].

[38]CPU (Central Processing Unit) – central processing and control unit of a computer.

[39]GPU (Graphics Processing Unit) – graphic processor of a computer.

[40]Application Specific Integrated Circuits.

[41]Joule per gigahash.

[42]Terahashes per second.

[43]Hash rate or computing power – how many hashing operations can be carried out in one second.

[44]Mishra, Sailendra Prasanna. "Bitcoin Mining And Its Cost." 2017.

their computing capacity. The upgrading of mining hardware continues, which further leads to a continuous increase in electricity consumption.

A potential attacker (like any other user) would have to solve the task with the same level of difficulty and likewise bear the "losses" of expended energy resources to create a valid block.

To forge one of the blocks that has already been added to the blockchain, an attacker would need to recalculate all of the other blocks as well. Because even a small change in a block leads to a new hash, the references in the blocks would no longer be correct. To successfully manipulate the block content, the attacker would need to control over 51 percent of the computing power of the entire Bitcoin network.

4.1.4   New Blockchains and Alternatives

Because Bitcoin, Ethereum and many other blockchain projects are open source projects, systems with different technical parameters are available for duplication and modification. In this case, the already mentioned term "fork" plays an important role. Any modification to an existing blockchain system (blockchain protocol) that leads to changes in defined rules and parameters (e.g. block time, block size, etc.) is referred to as a fork (e.g. Bitcoin fork). The two resulting branches have the same first block (genesis block) at the point of branching and the same predecessor blocks.

There are two types of blockchain forking: a hard fork and a soft fork. In the case of the hard fork, changes in the software must be accepted by all users (for instance, a change in the architecture of the blockchain: e.g. increasing the block size from 1 to 2 MB). Several hard forks have already been implemented on the Ethereum blockchain. The first took place on July 20, 2016. This is because a month earlier, due to an attack, an error was found in The DAO Framework[45] and 3.6 million Ether (65 million euros) were stolen. The Ethereum developers tracked down the error and decided on a hard fork as a means of regaining the stolen Ether. A soft fork affects changes in the blockchain, for instance new or updated functionalities that only need to be accepted by the majority of miners, as well as by the users, who want to use them. In contrast to a hard fork, a soft fork is backwards compatible.

In this way, many new applications with adapted parameters or new functionalities are created using, for example, Bitcoin blockchain. The question arises as to what extent this is still a blockchain. Can we only call the Bitcoin blockchain with its parameters and goals a blockchain, or does the term only apply to a cryptographically referenced chain of blocks? The hype surrounding the topic of blockchain plays a fundamental role here, as numerous technical concepts and projects, which already existed before blockchain technology and have little to do

---

[45]The DAO (Decentralized Autonomous Organization) implemented on the Ethereum blockchain. More about this can be found in Sect. 5.1.2.

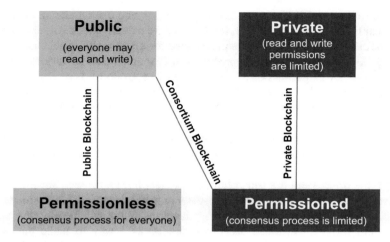

Fig. 4.8 Public and private Blockchain

with its innovation, experience higher sales when marketed under the blockchain name.

To find out what added value and what challenges blockchain technology brings us now – when compared to existing technological concepts – we see that definition plays a decisive role. For instance, in the next attempt to adapt blockchain technology to specific needs, namely the private and/or permissioned blockchain.

In doing so, we move away from the original ideas and goals of the Bitcoin and Ethereum blockchain and return to the limitation of user rights. The blockchain system consequently no longer remains completely decentralized, but is instead limited to predetermined users.[46] The terminology of so-called "blockchain types" are no more clearly defined than the term blockchain itself. A combination of the following use restrictions plays a role:

- Read permission – Who can see the blockchain contents,
- Write permission – Who can create transactions,
- Consensus permission – Who can update the blockchain (combining transactions into a block and adding the block to the chain) (Fig. 4.8).

These restrictions mean that users have to authenticate and authorize themselves to use the system [32]. In a private blockchain, also called a private permissioned blockchain, read and write permissions are limited to a group of users (e.g., in the area of a company or distributed over several companies). Thereby the transparency of the blockchain history is lost. The permission to update the blockchain is also limited to predefined users. In private blockchains, changes to the system are easier

---

[46]Often instead of referring to a "private" or "permissioned" blockchain, the term Distributed Ledger Technology (DLT) is used by the media.

and faster to carry out. This is because the users – who can update and verify the blockchain – are known. However, the risk of a 51 percent attack still exists, albeit in a modified form. Users, who are preselected for updating the blockchain and for participation in consensus finding process, can be manipulated by various attackers.

If the consensus permission is only limited to a group of users and every user has read permission, one speaks of a consortium blockchain or public permissioned blockchain. Write permission can either be given to all users or only to a certain group.

In the Bitcoin or Ethereum system, we speak of a public blockchain or also public permissionless blockchain (i.e., an original blockchain without restrictions in the terms of use).

Both the private and the consortium blockchain have their own advantages and disadvantages. These are reflected to a greater or lesser degree depending on the area of application. The intention of restricting the terms of use, and thereby centralizing the system for predetermined users, is intended as a way to make the system more efficient. The decentralization of the system is in this way secondary. It is often forgotten that the original goal of the first blockchain projects (e.g., Bitcoin) was a decentralized and secure electronic payment system, and that there was no intention of creating a competitor in the area of transaction throughput to the level of efficiency found in payment systems such as Visa or PayPal.

Therefore, a blockchain-based system in its "original form" (public permissionless blockchain) makes sense when a system is involved in which numerous users, who neither know nor trust each other want to interact. Trust in a central authority or in any kind of middlemen is not a prerequisite. Otherwise, a normal database is often the better way to go [32].

4.2   Challenges of Blockchain Technology

After looking at the technical foundations of blockchain technology, which combines already existing technical approaches (see Chap. 3) in an innovative form (see Sect. 4.1), we would now like to take a look at the challenges.

4.2.1   Possible Attacks

With the dissolution of the central authority of the trusted third party, the problem of a lack of trust between users arises. This problem is solved in decentralized systems using various methods, for example:

- Unambiguous user identification (e.g., a video identification procedure; the prerequisite is disclosure of one's own identity),
- Trust networks (prerequisite: mutual trust of at least one user in the system),

- Mutual evaluation of the users (prerequisite: majority of the users must be "honest"),
- Game-theoretical approaches (prerequisite/assumption: the users' behavior is completely determined by the underlying game or its rules, with the objective exclusively profit/win-oriented [9]).

It is important to strike a balance between security and usability (whether the use of the services is linked to certain conditions). If the use of a decentralized system is not dependent on certain conditions, then the likelihood of a Sybil attack increases. The name of this attack method comes from the main character of a book[47] by Flora Rheta Schreiber. The book describes Sybil, a woman with multiple personalities. Similar to the case in the book, the attacker in a decentralized system creates many false "identities" (nodes, servers) to manipulate or disrupt communication in the system [70]. In this case, it is important that the honest users make up the majority.

In a blockchain-based system, attackers can generally only forward selected blocks and transactions, and in this way shut out other users from the network. The Bitcoin system attempts to prevent this type of attack by restricting outgoing connections (see also Sect. 3.2).

Because blockchain technology assumed that in a system without participation conditions,[48] the majority of resources[49] is in the hands of honest users and not that the majority of users are honest, a malicious user cannot influence the consensus only using a Sybil attack as long as the user does not have a majority of resources.

If an attacker in a PoW-based blockchain system has more than 50 percent of the total computing capacity of the system,[50] the following manipulations of the blockchain are possible:

- Monopolizing the mining of new blocks, and thereby keeping the reward exclusively,
- Asserting the own blockchain as the longest chain,
- Only including blocks of the own transactions or blocking the transactions of certain users (not including them in the blocks),
- Carrying out double-spending.[51] In block creation, the miner must check whether the values were already "spent" in previous transactions (thus, who is the current owner). The attacker can ignore this rule in block creation and re-use his already issued values multiple times.

This procedure is also known as the 51 percent attack. To change earlier blocks, the attacker must recalculate the entire chain (blockchain) from the block to be changed (thus, recalculate all previous blocks up to the first block). In this case,

---

[47]"Sybil" was written in 1973 by Flora Rheta Schreiber.

[48]Malicious users can create many false identities.

[49]Computing power in a PoW, "account credit" in PoS.

[50]More computing capacity as all of the other users together.

[51]More on this subject can be found in the [31].

the attacker can only change the order of transactions in the chain or remove them from the chain [2].

Lightweight users (lightweight nodes) do not have a complete blockchain and cannot guarantee a complete verification of the transaction contents. They must therefore trust the miner and are accordingly not as secure as full nodes [67]. Both concepts, PoW and PoS, are thus vulnerable to the 51 percent attack.

Such an attack can devour a lot of money in the Bitcoin system. According to BTCECHO, such an attack could cost the attacker approx. 375.2 million euros per day [86]. Profit-oriented attackers thus prefer a cheaper alternative.

In the Bitcoin system, mining pools have the largest share of the total computing capacity (more on this subject can be found in [79]).

In July 2014, the mining pool Ghash.io gained more than 50 percent of the computing capacity of the entire Bitcoin network. The Bitcoin community responded by introducing certain restrictions. There is currently an agreement between the mining pools in place not to exceed the 39.99 percent limit. Additionally, a supervisory committee has been set up to monitor the computing power of the mining pools. It is made up of representatives of the mining pools and of Bitcoin companies as well as other specialists from this sector [199].

Nevertheless, the possibility remains that an attack can be carried out with less computing power than 50 percent of the entire network. The success rate is, however, correspondingly low [31].

Under no circumstances can an attacker use the 51 percent attack to generate new values (e.g., bitcoins, through rewards) or redirect values from transactions of other users to himself. This is only possible if the attacker has access to the private key of the respective user (the corresponding user address[52]) [2]. With minimal effort and standard tools, attackers can spy out the private key of a user, if the user is inadequately protected. For this reason for example, it is recommended that Bitcoin users not use online services that offer online wallets. Recently, these have suffered from security vulnerabilities that make it possible for attackers to steal users' bitcoins [53].

Applications that are installed locally at the user's computer promise more security for storing the private keys. Many of them offer wallet encryption and regular backups. A two-factor authentication makes the storage of the private keys more secure. Thereby, the identity of the user is checked by proof of two components – for example a combination of hardware wallet and PIN or password. The private keys are stored on an external data medium that needs a PIN or a password for unlocking and is immune against viruses. The private key never leaves the storage medium. The transactions are processed within the data carrier. The transactions are signed using the corresponding private key. After this is done, the signed transactions are transferred to the application on the user computer [60].

Unlike private keys, public keys are used for generating addresses ("Pay-to-Public-Key-Hash" or "Pay-to-Script-Hash" addresses – see Sect. 3.1.2). The

---

[52]See Sect. 3.1.2.

addresses which are, for example, generated specifically for each new transaction in the Bitcoin system, can be linked to the end users, despite the use of the TOR network. In the scientific work of Biryukov and Pustogarov from 2014 [4], such a method for the de-anonymization of Bitcoin users was described. The Bitcoin addresses and the IP addresses of senders were connected. The method also works if users have a firewall or use the TOR network. Based on this information, changes have been made in other versions of Bitcoin [27]. While mixing services (see Sect. 3.2.1) offer more anonymity, they also require trust in the provider of such services.

It is important to note that the IP addresses of many full nodes are public, which makes the assigning of completed transaction to the user easier. An attacker can take advantage of another attack option with the public IP address of a full node – namely, DoS[53] attacks. Here, a targeted overload of a network node (e.g., a full node) is carried out. Afterwards, the user can no longer provide his service as intended. Overloading can occur when a huge number of messages are sent to the victim. In this way, so many resources are tied up that the victim becomes overloaded and can no longer carry out the actual work at hand.

To ward off such attacks, Bitcoin implements a reputation-based rule: every user who sends a faulty or manipulated message receives penalty points. If the number of these points reaches 100, the IP address is blocked for 24 hours [4]. Because the attack can originate from multiple IP addresses (e.g., from a botnet), Bitcoin sets further rules to protect against DoS attacks. Among these rule are:

- Do not forward orphan transactions and blocks to other users,
- Do not forward transactions whose content (bitcoins) has already been used up (double-spend transactions),
- A message that has already been sent to a user (transaction, block, address of another user) may not be sent twice,
- The block size may not exceed 1 MB.

Another rule protects the Bitcoin system against spam transactions or so-called flood attacks. In this case, the attacker creates several transactions addressed to himself. This is done with the aim of filling a new block with his own transactions and delaying the addition of transactions from other users. The attacker does not charge any transaction fees. However, the Bitcoin system only allows five percent of free transaction in blocks. This means that an attack is then only possible when the attacker is prepared to waste his bitcoins to carry it out [67].

The intention of developing new blockchain systems and designing them for new uses leads to ever more changes and adaptations of the original Bitcoin code. This can result in security gaps as well as other potential attacks. For example, smart contracts present autonomous programs that users can design and run on their computers. These can, for example, exhibit security vulnerabilities due to program errors (more on this subject can be found in the article [21]). In 2016, scientists at the

---

[53]Denial of Service.

National University of Singapore described in their research work "Making Smart Contracts Smarter" that approximately 45 percent of Ethereum smart contracts contain errors[54] and thus could exhibit security gaps.

The source code of many blockchain-based systems is public and continuously analyzed by multiple IT experts for weaknesses and subsequently improved. In the past few years, no serious security-related vulnerabilities have been found in the Bitcoin system [58, 67]. However, many more changes have been made and will be made to protect the Bitcoin system against attacks. The cryptographic algorithms used in most blockchain-based systems (Bitcoin, Ethereum, etc.) are at this time among the best. Of course there is a risk that these could be manipulated in the future [138]. The developers, however, promise to switch to better algorithms when that danger becomes real [67].

4.2.2 Scalability

The ability to scale is one of the most important properties of decentralized networks. It is measured by how the performance varies when the system is re-sized and whether the system can grow without loss.

With the increasing popularity of blockchain technology, more and more users are joining systems such as Bitcoin or Ethereum. New users mean a bigger transaction volume for the system. In 2016, there were, for example, around 40,000 transactions per day for Ethereum (Fig. 4.9) and approximately 236,000 transactions for Bitcoin (Fig. 4.10) added to the blockchain, and at the beginning of 2020 there were already 600,000 for Ethereum and 320,000 for Bitcoin [77, 114]. The Bitcoin system can currently process up to 7 transactions per second and Ethereum up to 20.

In Sect. 4.1.4 we have indicated that not every system that has blockchain in its name is in fact based on blockchain technology. In an attempt to adapt blockchain technology to fit one's own needs and make it "more efficient," either the decentralization or the security of the system gets lost. In this context, we often speak about the so-called scalability trilemma (Fig. 4.11).[55]

If we, for instance, only have a few full nodes in our system and the rest of the system consists of lightweight users[56] (lightweight nodes), the possible centralization of the system also implies the risk of a security loss.[57]

---

[54]Errors examined in the paper [22].

[55]This term comes from Vitalik Buterin co-founder of Ethereum.

[56]Lightweight users only store the block header and the information that applies to their transactions. Because the lightweight users do not have any block contents (transactions), they have to trust the full nodes that the blocks and transactions are created in accordance with the rules and do not contain any doubled spending.

[57]The few full nodes could also possibly agree, for example, to manipulate the system by double-spending.

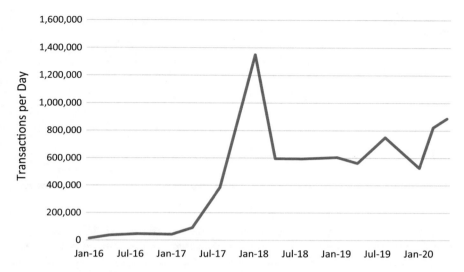

Fig. 4.9 Ethereum: Transactions per day [73, 114, 115]

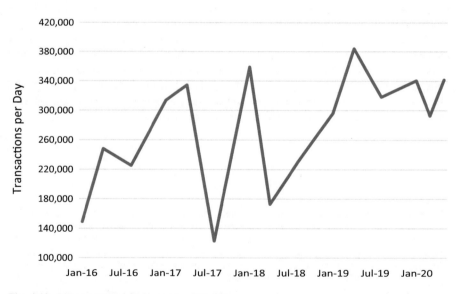

Fig. 4.10 Bitcoin: Transactions per day [72, 77]

Fig. 4.11 Scalability
trilemma

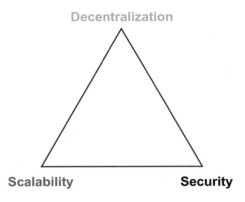

In terms of efficiency, a blockchain-based system (PoW-based public blockchain) can therefore not compete with a comparable, centralized solution such as Hyperledger Fabric[58] or Ripple[59] (which use a permissioned blockchain) with their thousands of transactions per second [32]. This is not because blockchain technology is still new and unoptimized, but stems from the nature of the technology itself [32]. Public permissionless blockchain projects, such as Bitcoin and Ethereum[60] use Proof-of-Work to ensure a robust and secure decentralized system.[61]

The level of difficulty of a Proof-of-Work task depends on the parameters, such as the block time, and is adjusted accordingly so that a predetermined time is always required to create a block. In the Bitcoin system this is 10 minutes and in the Ethereum system between 12 and 15 seconds [132]. If the computing power of the entire network increases or decreases and the block generation time changes, then the level of difficulty is correspondingly raised or lowered.

---

[58]Hyperledger is an open source consortium founded in December 2015 by the Linux Foundation to advance cross-industry blockchain applications. In 2017, there were approximately 170 members. It is a global collaboration of leading companies from the areas of finance, banking, the Internet of Things, supply chains, manufacturing and technology with over 400 programmers. The Hyperledger consortium is one of the fastest growing cooperation projects of the Linux Foundation. Hyperledger supports several projects in different areas of application to guarantee the interoperability of numerous blockchain business solutions. Currently, the consortium provides five open source blockchain frameworks and four open source blockchain tools with smart contracts, client libraries, graphical interfaces and sample applications. With the help of these frameworks and tools, companies can implement blockchain technology-based applications and services for their business sectors [140].

[59]More on this subject in Chap. 6.

[60]Ethereum developers have been working on a Proof-of-Stake solution for years. The first phase of the changeover should take place in 2020.

[61]The users of the system "vote" on the correctness of the system with their computing power.

If the block time is reduced in order to raise the system's productivity,[62] or, more precisely, the transaction throughput, the security of the system becomes vulnerable. Generally-speaking, a shorter block time means a higher fork rate, which in turn means that a higher number of confirmations is required (in the Bitcoin system, a transaction is only considered confirmed after 6 blocks). A higher fork rate also means that more work is wasted [17, 32]. Ethereum solves the problem of the shorter block time (between 12 and 15 seconds) using the modified GHOST protocol [33, 127], in which orphan blocks[63] are included into the calculation of the "longest chain" and the miners of these blocks rewarded.

The block size presents a further limitation. Besides determining the block time and transaction throughput, it also ensures the security in a public permissionless blockchain system. In the Bitcoin system the block size is 1 MB. To raise the block size would mean blocks having longer propagation and confirmation times, which in turn could lead to an increased fork rate and double-spending attacks [127]. Therefore, as with Ethereum, the block size must be correspondingly smaller to allow a secure and fast distribution of blocks within 15 seconds [32]. In contrast to Bitcoin, the Ethereum block size is not defined and is based on the complexity of smart contracts. This is known as gasLimit (see Sect. 4.1.1) per transaction. The gasLimits of the transactions included in a block are added and their total constitutes the gasLimit for the respective block. The maximum gasLimit for a block is determined by an algorithm[64] and by a consensus of the miners [128]. Miners are allowed to change the maximum gasLimit for a block by 0.0975 percent of the gasLimit of the previous block [128]. Therefore, the maximum block size in Ethereum can vary slightly from block to block [74]. In May 2020, the block size in the Ethereum system was approximately 27 kB [112].

The Bitcoin community has long discussed whether the block size should remain at 1 MB or be increased to 2 MB. Such fundamental changes in the protocol, for example block size or block time, require a hard fork. Because a hard fork must be accepted by all miners and all users, those who do not accept these changes and do not update them are "split off" from the system. Neither the Bitcoin developers nor the miners can force users to accept new changes that violate existing system rules, this is due to the design of the system. This means that developers can only hope that the new changes will be accepted by many miners and users [190].

A new cryptocurrency called Bitcoin Cash (BCH) was created through such a split on August 1, 2017. It introduced 8 MB blocks and split the Bitcoin system. Another group in the Bitcoin community chose to take a different path in solving the block size problem. On August 24 of the same year, through a soft fork as part of

---

[62]The term scalability is often associated with productivity. If productivity is maintained when the system is resized the system is considered to be scalable [15].

[63]In Ethereum jargon called "uncles." Only "uncles" up to the 7th generation are considered [127].

[64]Ethereum-Yellow-Paper [38, 111].

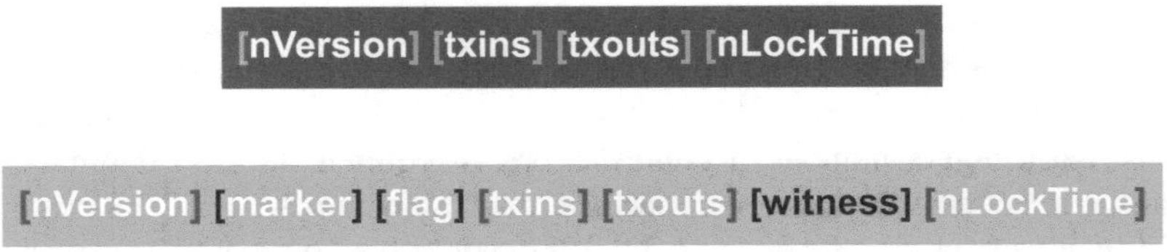

[nVersion] [txins] [txouts] [nLockTime]

[nVersion] [marker] [flag] [txins] [txouts] [witness] [nLockTime]

Fig. 4.12 General format of a Bitcoin transaction before BIP141 and after

the BIP 141[65] [125], a number of innovations for better scalability under the name "Segregated Witness," SegWit for short, was introduced in the Bitcoin system. The advantage over the hard fork is that users can be updated at any time, after the miners have accepted the changes. This means that the miners and the users, who have not yet updated the new functionalities, continue to belong to the same system as the updated users. They only see one "extra text" they do not understand, however this does not pose a problem as it does not mean any changes to the fundamental rules [188–190].

The focus of BIP 141 is on a new data structure called Witness. A part of the transaction is "moved," therein, namely the signature, which otherwise makes up to 70 percent of a transaction.

At this point, let us look back at the technical foundation described above and recall the "structure" of the Bitcoin transaction (see Sect. 4.1.1). A Bitcoin transaction consists of one or more inputs and outputs. In the input we have a Bitcoin value (the hash of a previous transaction, also called the transaction ID, and a corresponding output index) and its unlocking mechanism (ScriptSig). The output includes:

- what part of the value is to be transmitted as well as
- a locking mechanism with a series of instructions describing how the owner of the respective recipient address can gain access to the value (ScriptPubKey).

Thus "Witness" still remains part of the transaction (see Fig. 4.12), but is not hashed in the transaction ID. Therefore, users[66] who have not yet implemented SegWit think that SegWit transactions do not have a signature (in the ScriptSig) and do not require one (in the ScriptPubKey). The updated users understand the instructions in the ScriptPubKey and know that the necessary signature is in the "Witness area." Because both updated and non-updated users see the same transaction ID, they agree to the structure and format of the transaction. For greater

---

[65]Bitcoin Improvement Proposal (BIP) is a design document for the introduction of functions or information in Bitcoin [56].

[66]Full nodes including miners.

security, the miners, who have implemented the SegWit, add a Merkle root[67] of the "Witness signatures" to the input of the coinbase transaction[68] [188].

The question might arise as to what extent a SegWit update solves the scalability problem of the Bitcoin system and, specifically, how the size of the transaction is decreased if "Witness" still remains a part of the transaction. The block size limit in the Bitcoin system remains unchanged after the SegWit update at 1 MB. Block size is replaced by "block weight," and the block can have a "weight" of between 2 and 4 MB. This means, the current full nodes need more time than before to verify a block. This correspondingly increases the block's spread time in the system. SegWit supporters consider the additional verification time and the associated longer propagation time for a block of individual nodes (full nodes) as low, and that it lies within the limits of what the network can currently handle [190]. The debate about the "efficient" block size therefore continues. Other experts within the Bitcoin community are of the opinion that the 2 to 4 MB size blocks are still not sufficient to reach the desired transaction throughput and to make the Bitcoin system competitive, when compared to centralized solutions.

On the other hand, SegWit is paving the way for new opportunities that could improve the flexibility, security and scalability of the Bitcoin system in the near future. Only a few of these are Version bytes, Merkelized Abstract Syntax Trees (MAST), the Schnorr cryptographic signature algorithm, and Lightning Network.

A so-called version byte encodes the unlocking mechanism type ("ScriptSig type").[69] In the Witness area we find the following:

- Pay to Witness Public Key Hash (P2WPKH):[70] Signature and matching public key,
- Pay to Witness Script Hash (P2WSH):[71] Script and the necessary data for implementation (public keys and signatures) (Figs. 4.13 and 4.14).

Let's imagine that Alice wants to "transfer" two bitcoins to Bob. Bob plans that these bitcoins only be spent by his children when they reach the age of 18. Bob creates two private keys, of which, with the help of ECDSA (Elliptic Curve Digital Signature Algorithm, see Sect. 3.1.2.) he receives a public key for each. Bob creates a script which states that his daughter Bea (first public key) will be allowed to use half of the bitcoins starting in 2025.[72] It also states that his son Bill (second public key) gets the second half starting in 2030. Finally, Bob takes the script with the public keys used there and creates a hash value. Since both Bob and Alice have

---

[67] See Sect. 4.1.3.

[68] The first transaction in the block, which pays the mining reward (see Sect. 4.1.3).

[69] Version Byte defines a number. This number is followed by a hash value. This hash value is either from a public key and is 20 bytes long (Pay to Witness Public Key Hash address) or from a script and is 32 bytes long (Pay to Witness Script Hash address).

[70] Version byte is 0 and 20 bytes hash.

[71] Version byte is 0 and 32 bytes hash.

[72] Assuming that in 2025 she will be 18 years old.

witness:	0 <signature1> <1 <pubkey1> <pubkey2> 2 CHECKMULTISIG>
scriptSig:	(empty)
scriptPubKey:	0 <20-byte-key-hash>

Fig. 4.13 Pay to Witness Public Key Hash – BIP141 [59, 125]

witness:	0 <signature1> <1 <pubkey1> <pubkey2> 2 CHECKMULTISIG>
scriptSig:	(empty)
scriptPubKey:	0 <32-byte-hash>

Fig. 4.14 Pay to Witness Script Hash – BIP141 [59, 125]

already implemented SegWit updates, Alice uses Bob's P2WSH address. This is a 32-byte hash value, which Bob generated, and a version byte 0 at the beginning. This information appears in the ScriptPubKey in the output of Alice's transaction. Bea can thus use her private key (the private key that corresponds to her public key) to "spend" her bitcoin starting in 2025. To do this, she would create a transaction whose ScriptSig is empty, and contains the following information in the Witness area: version byte 0, her signature (generated by means of her private key) and the script with the public key used there.

In the future, bitcoins can be blocked by various scripts, which developers can design in desired fashion and that can be introduced at any time as a soft fork. For example, a P2WSH address version byte 1 with a subsequent 32-byte hash value would mean that the bitcoins to be "transferred" are "locked out" by a mechanism called the Merkelized Abstract Syntax Tree (MAST for short). Two approaches that we are already familiar with: the Pay-to-Script hash and the Merkle Tree, are put together using an abstract syntax tree technology. An abstract syntax tree, as the name implies, allows a script to be composed in the form of a tree. The individual instructions and the data of the script represent the "leaves" of the tree. These are hashed together to form a Merkle root (see Sect. 4.1.2). The Merkle root is then used in the form of a 32-byte hash as the P2WSH address.

In the case of a P2SH or a P2WSH address, a script is usually listed in full in the ScriptSig or Witness area. If we think back to our example with Alice and Bob, this means that in 2030 Bill must list the complete script in his Witness area besides his signature (even when Bea has already spend her bitcoin, therefore already listed the script in her transaction). If Bob had used the MAST concept, instead of simply hashing the script, Bill would only have to use his part of the script and a hash of Bea's script. This would have several advantages, such as data protection and improved scalability. The information from Bea's script is, for example, not revealed in the bill transaction. Because it is only one hash value, the transaction is correspondingly smaller.

By moving the signature (in a multi-signature script – multiple signatures) to the Witness area, the use of a new signature algorithms is possible. Such is the case with the application of a so-called Schnorr signature. Flexibility, security and scalability of the Bitcoin system can be thereby improved. The inputs of a transaction, which are otherwise individually signed using the Elliptic Curve Digital Signature algorithm (ECDSA) can be signed together by means of a Schnorr signature. This leaves much more space for more diverse scripts, which may be similar in their complexity to the Ethereum scripts [191].

Indeed, the Ethereum system has to struggle with a larger amount of data than the Bitcoin system. As in every public permissionless blockchain system, every Ethereum full node bears the entire transaction load. This means carrying out and storing every transaction in the blockchain history [32, 134]. The transactions and the scripts contained therein (smart contracts) are highly complex. In this sense, the account-based Ethereum system has a considerable advantage over the UTXO-based Bitcoin system. When verifying a transaction, the entire blockchain is no longer searched for an output, which is referenced in the current input. Instead, the current state of the respective account (account state) is checked as to whether it has a sufficient balance [38, 64]. The full nodes, who store the entire history of the account states are called archive nodes and are rare, and there is talk about whether or not they are even necessary. A conventional Ethereum full node[73] only saves the current states and deletes the old[74] [120]. This, however, does not offer a long-term solution for the problem potential centralization. The larger the blockchain is, the fewer users there are who can afford to remain full nodes.

In order to improve the scalability and security of the Ethereum system for the long term and to continue to ensure decentralization, Ethereum developers plan to create and introduce an Ethereum 2.0 within the next two to three years.[75] The focus is on splitting the entire system into numerous groups and thus dividing the transaction load and allowing parallel calculations. Let us take one of the example from Vitalik Buterin[76] on this topic and imagine that the Ethereum system is divided into thousands of islands. Each island has its own functionalities. The inhabitants (users and smart contracts with their accounts) of an island communicate with each other, organize themselves, have their own transaction history and carry out their own transactions. The islands can interact with each other. This procedure is called sharding and the "islands" are correspondingly called "shards." Sharding is a term that was originally comes from the database field[77] and was adapted by the Ethereum developers in the Ethereum system.

---

[73]Ethereum client settings: Geth full or Parity no-warp (for more on this topic see [121]).

[74]State tree pruning.

[75]By 2022. For more information on this subject, see the Ethereum Roadmap Appendix F.

[76]Co-founder of Ethereum.

[77]Sharding is a scaling method used in the area of databases. Data in a database is thereby split up into multiple shards and stored and managed on different servers.

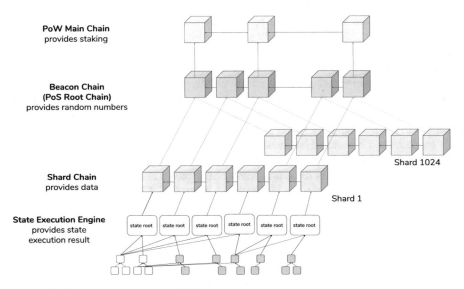

Fig. 4.15 Ethereum 2.0 architecture [139]

The entire architecture of the Ethereum system is thereby "rebuilt" and can be displayed in several layers. The shards represent the two lowest layers of this new architecture: the data and execution layers (see Fig. 4.15). The transactions and smart contracts are executed and saved for each shard. The next layer is used to coordinate and validate the data produced in the shards. This layer consists of a new blockchain – a so-called beacon chain, which uses a PoS algorithm (in Ethereum Casper protocol). Miners are replaced by validators, which using the PoS algorithm have the possibility to create a block in a shard that has been randomly assigned to them. For each shard, a group made up of 100^{78} randomly selected validators, authenticate the new block by signing (attesting). The block header is included in the beacon chain block with at least 67 signatures as references to the shard block [108, 116, 117, 168].

The current Ethereum blockchain remains available, uses PoW and represents a top layer. Any Ethereum user who stores 32 Ether in the form of a smart contract in the Ethereum blockchain (top layer) can be a validator.

Ethereum 2.0 is an attempt to solve the scalability trilemma. In this way, the scalability of the Ethereum system should be greatly improved without sacrificing security and decentralization.

Up to now, we have looked at possible scaling solutions that make the existing blockchain system more efficient through the adaptation of existing parameters and the addition of new functionalities. A further scaling option intended to relieve the

---

[78] Because Ethereum 2.0 is still under development at the time of this writing, some implementation details given here may differ from those expressed at a later date.

system takes the form of so-called off-chain transactions. As the name suggests, the transactions are carried out outside of the blockchain and thus not registered in the blockchain. Here, we are again reminded of the scalability trilemma. Indeed, the security of the system can be compromised because the transactions are no longer verified in the network. Both Bitcoin and Ethereum are working on possible secure off-chain solutions:

- Micropayment channels (or payment channels),
- State channels,
- Child chains,
- Side chains.

We have previously touched on the problem of long transaction confirmation times and rising transaction fees in the Bitcoin system. A Bitcoin transaction is first then considered valid when it is included in a block that already has at least five successor blocks. As every new block is created in ten minutes, the waiting time is at least one hour. Since miners receive the transaction fees of all transactions included in the block, they prefer transactions with higher fees. This means that the higher the transaction fee, the faster the transaction will be included in a new block. Thus, a small payment with bitcoins can be subject to a relatively long waiting time – a disadvantage that can be remedied by off-chain transactions. Temporary micropayment channels are created between the users. As long as the channel is open, users can exchange transactions in large numbers and do so at high speed. After expiration of the agreed time, these transactions (or a sum total transaction) are released for the blockchain. Micropayment channels are already in use in the Bitcoin system. A slightly adapted example of this procedure from Bitcon.org offers further insight on the subject [51].

Imagine that Bob is a digital nomad and operates a website with helpful tips for budget backpacking trips. His website includes an online forum that needs to be maintained around the clock. Bob has hired Alice to take care of the forum. Every time someone writes something in Bob's forum, Alice is notified and can check the post to make sure it doesn't violate forum policy guidelines. Bob wants to pay Alice immediately after each verified post and uses Bitcoin's micropayment option to do this. Bob asks Alice for her public key and then creates two transactions. In the first transaction, Bob pays 90 millibitcoins to the P2SH address. The script at this address requires signatures from Alice and Bob to unlock the bitcoins. There is a transaction fee of 10 millibitcoins. This transaction is called a bond transaction. If Bob were to immediately send the transaction to the blockchain network, Alice could choose not to do any work and not to sign the next transaction[79] that unlocks the bitcoins. Consequently, Bob could also not do anything with these bitcoins, and he therefore initially keeps the transaction. In the second

(continued)

transaction (the so-called refund transaction), 80 millibitcoins from the first transaction are refunded to Bob after 24 hours have expired,[80] the remaining 10 millibitcoins are transaction fees. Since the refund transaction "issues" the bitcoins from the bond transaction, they can only be unlocked with the signatures of Bob and Alice. Bob gives Alice the refund transaction to sign. Alice reviews the transaction, determines that it has a 24-hour lockout period and keeps a copy of it. She sends the signed transaction back to Bob and asks him about the bond transaction. Bob then forwards it to Alice and keeps the copy. Alice checks if the references between the refund and bond transaction are correct. She can now send the bond transaction to the Bitcoin network to lock the millibitcoins. Bob in turn has received the refund transaction that is already signed by Alice. He knows that if Alice does not do any work, he can send the transaction to the network and get back his millibitcoins that are locked for 24 hours.

After Alice has processed the first forum posts, she asks Bob for payment. Bob creates a new refund transaction without a lockout period.[81] The input remains unchanged. Bob transfers 1 millibitcoin to Alice in an output and in another output 79 millibitcoins to himself. Ten millibitcoins remain as transaction fees. Bob signs this transaction and send it to Alice. Thus, Alice has the possibility to sign and spend the transaction whenever she wants. She keeps it and continues to work. After further checked forum posts, the procedure is repeated and a new version of the refund transaction is created and signed. When Alice has finished her work for the day and is not going to process any further posts that day, or shortly before the lockout period expires, she signs the last version of the refund transaction and sends it to the Bitcoin network. Bob and Alice create a new micropayment channel next workday.

---

[79]More specifically, the input that refers to the output of the bond transaction and lists the script.

[80]In the input of this transaction, the output from the bond transaction is referenced and the multi-signature script with the signatures of Alice and Bob is listed. In the output, the bitcoins are locked for 24 hours.

[81]He keeps the first version of the refund transaction that was already signed by Alice and Bob for security reasons.

The idea of micropayment channels was further pursued by Joseph Poon and Thaddeus Dryja in their 2016 work, "The Bitcoin Lightning Network: Scalable Off-Chain Instant Payments." This work describes a concept for a network of micropayment channels for the Bitcoin system. The concept allows for scalable and

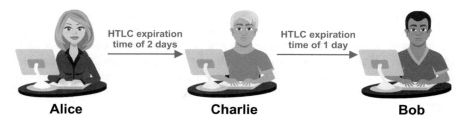

Fig. 4.16 Network of micropayment channels

immediately executable off-chain transactions, bidirectional payment channels,[82] a large network of micropayment channels,[83] low fees for the bidirectional channels[84] and a possibility to exchange cryptocurrencies between different blockchains (so called atomic swaps). The first implementation of the Lightning Network for Bitcoin system "Ind" has been in place since January 2017 [154].

In the Ethereum system, the use of Lightning Network technology is called the "Raiden" Network. It allows the virtually instantaneous, fee-free, scalable and confidential exchange of values[85] [166]. Similar to the micropayment or payment channels, the next off-chain solution of the Ethereum system are known as state channels. Thereby, the states outside of the blockchain are updated instead of the values [118].

A chess game between Alice and Bob provides an example of this situation. Instead of sending a new transaction with the state update to the Ethereum network after every chess move, the states are updated in a state channel. Only the last transaction is sent to the network [118].

---

[82]Recalling our online forum example, in this case the bond transaction can be "financed" by Alice and Bob's and either of them can close the channel by transferring the latest version of the update transaction to the blockchain.

[83]In the Lightning Network, a secure transaction exchange is also possible between two users who do not have an open micropayment channel between them. A path across several network nodes (users) is found (similar to routing on the Internet through multiple hops). The technology that allows this is called Hashed Timelock Contracts (HTLC). For example, Alice has an open channel with Charlie, and Charlie in turn with Bob. Alice and Bob want to exchange off-chain transactions. Then Alice requests a hash from Bob and counts the nodes (users) between both. Depending on the number of nodes (there is only one node between Alice and Bob – Charlie), it sets an HTLC expiration time of two days. Charlie sets the HTLC expiration time with Bob to 1 day. Bob shares the hash value with Charlie and in this way both agree to exchange small transactions. Charlie and Alice go through the same process (see Fig. 4.16) [30].

[84]The fees in the Lightning Network are very small and are paid between the two users communicating in the channel.

[85]ERC20 compliant token.

Another off-chain scalability solution in the Ethereum system is called "Plasma." It facilitates smaller "child" or "side" chains based on the Ethereum blockchain. This means that not only updating the states can be done outside the main blockchain, but also that solutions are much more complex. Within the framework of a smart contract (on the Ethereum blockchain), the parties agree on the content and rules in the new child chain. They can implement their own validation and fraud prevention mechanisms (Proof-of-Work, Proof-of-Stake, Proof-of-Authority) and have additional child chains [119].

As already mentioned, while off-chain scaling solutions relieve the system, they far from provide the security of on-chain alternatives. We therefore find ourselves once again at the scalability trilemma. With this in mind, we would like to close the chapter with the following thought: "The focus of blockchain technology is a robust and secure decentralized system without any conditions for the number of system users or their identification. Yet in an attempt to make the blockchain more efficient, the security or the decentralization of the system often suffers."

Chapter 5
The Right Use Leads to Success

Abstract What kind of problems can blockchain technology solve as an "ultimate" technology? Taking a sober look at a new technology is the basis for its potentially successful use. We would therefore like to concentrate on the innovation of blockchain technology and consider the advantages that this technology offers us when compared to already existing solutions, such as the distributed database. In this chapter we will look at the possibilities that have opened up due to blockchain technology and offer insights with the help of an example.

In 2016 and 2017, as the hype surrounding blockchain technology reached its peak, numerous companies took part in a "blockchain experiment" – an experiment because it involved a new technology, the definition of which is still being discussed today.[1] Numerous companies have attempted to make their processes more efficient through blockchain or by offering other companies an effective blockchain solution – each with its own idea of what the blockchain is. But contrary to expectations, this new, "ultimate" technology could not solve all the problems in the world, and the first doubts started to slowly surface as to whether blockchain could keep any of its promises at all. A sober consideration of a new technology is the cornerstone of its success, and this can only be carried out in the course of proper implementation.

We will therefore focus on the innovation of blockchain technology and consider the advantages that this technology offers compared to existing solutions, such as distributed databases. Imagine a random application with numerous users and/or parties that want to interact together but do not trust each other. Which of the following solutions would you consider for your application?

---

[1] At the time of the writing of this book.

© Springer Nature Switzerland AG 2021
T. Gayvoronskaya, C. Meinel, *Blockchain*,
https://doi.org/10.1007/978-3-030-61559-8_5

- A robust and highly efficient solution with limited user permissions (scalable and secure)[2] or
- a robust solution without intermediaries and a central authority (decentralized and secure).[3]

The first solution describes a private permissioned blockchain. Such a solution can often also be made possible by a distributed database system. The second solution uses a public permissionless blockchain.

When the central issue is the trust to be placed in a third party, we speak of a centralized system. For example, in an identity management system today we need one or more trustworthy verifiers who can verify and confirm the statement (claim) we make. Such a statement can be an address or the ownership of a driver's license. This can be done with the help of the public key infrastructure (PKI), which has been widely used for many years. In other cases, where trust is necessary, solutions such as the Web of Trust[4] or Proof-of-Authority[5] can be applied.

Let's assume you have decided on a robust solution without intermediaries and a central authority. The next step is to define additional criteria. These include the cost-benefit ratio (size of the system,[6] the existence of a separate IT team, transaction fees or gas costs[7] for existing public blockchain providers). Based on this, the decision is made whether you want to use an existing solution or if you want to develop your own. The next question concerns the actual objective, or more specifically the "content" of your application, namely: Which interactions are to take place between the users? Is the focus of your application on the fact that the state (or more precisely the possession of a value) must be securely recorded and logged? For example, in the case of the ownership of securities, an art object, a product[8] or the logging of copyrights. The ownership can additionally be linked to simple conditions, such as permission for a limited period of time.[9] For such purposes, a simple UTXO-based blockchain 1.0 is sufficient since the state of the values recorded means that they are either "unspent" or "spent."

---

[2]See scalability trilemma in Sect. 4.2.2.

[3]See scalability trilemma in Sect. 4.2.2.

[4]WOT – In a so-called network of trust, each user of the system can decide who he trusts and who he doesn't [6]. Such a network of trust enables a user to form an opinion about another user without having interacted with him before [14]. Various algorithms exist to implement such a system.

[5]PoA – a group of trustworthy validators secures the system. More information on the subject of PoA can be found in [8, 161].

[6]Number of possible users.

[7]A fee in the Ethereum system applied to each step in the calculation of a smart contract (see Sect. 4.1.1).

[8]For instance, a prescription drug whose path from the manufacturer via the pharmacist to the customer can be recorded in a way that is tamper-proof.

[9]For instance in the case of a cinema ticket. Imagine that seat 12A in your movie theater can "belong" to one of your visitors for a certain time period.

But if you want your application to be more complex, an account-based blockchain 2.0 is the better choice. This is the case, for example, if the states of a value or an individual user accounts need to offer greater flexibility, or if the interaction of your users is associated with complex conditions that are to be automatically controlled and executed. It not only enables a robust and secure decentralized system for the logging of the possession of a value, but the system also acts as a large decentralized computer with millions of autonomous objects. With the help of these autonomous objects (specifically, smart contracts), you can create any complex applications. These so-called decentralized applications, or dApps for short, can be controlled and used in a decentralized manner without further intermediaries. For instance, this could be a smart contract that regulates the rental of an apartment. When a potential tenant has paid to rent an apartment and the day of rental has arrived, a digital key[10] to unlock the apartment is sent to the tenant. The digital key is limited to the rental period. More complex smart contracts can represent so-called decentralized autonomous organizations (DAO) whose functions are executed automatically depending on predefined conditions.

Let's assume you have decided on one of the blockchain-based solutions (UTXO- or account-based solution). We will now take a closer look at the most widespread use methods of these solutions.

5.1   The Application of an Existing Blockchain Solution

Every company who wants to jump on the blockchain bandwagon should take a closer look at the cost-benefit ratio before deciding on an implementation. There are numerous projects and providers on the market that support companies in introducing blockchain. A company has to ultimately decide whether to pursue the development of its own blockchain or to use an existing one (e.g. Bitcoin or Ethereum).

Bitcoin and Ethereum have established themselves as standards on the blockchain scene and currently serve as the basis for many other applications.

5.1.1   UTXO-Based Solution with Colored Coins

By using colored coins it is possible to simply build one's own UTXO-based solution on an already existing blockchain system (such as Bitcoin).

The principle of "colored coins" involves adding to the already available values (i.e., to UTXO), for example bitcoins, additional information (metadata). By becoming linked to this information, the original Bitcoins become "colored" and

---

[10]For an electronic lock.

<table>
<tr><td>Metadata is added
to the Bitcoin</td><td>The Colored Coin is
signed with Alice's
private key</td><td>The Colored Coin
is available for
Alice to use</td></tr>
</table>

Fig. 5.1 Colored coins method based on the Bitcoin blockchain with a new value (apartment for rent)

acquire a different semantic/use. For example, they can represent a new value such as a certificate, a share of a stock, a movie ticket, a rental apartment or a digital key for a house or a car (see Fig. 5.1) [126].

The users who exchange colored coins use a colored coins application and know what value or what property the coins have. However, the blockchain miners cannot recognize the "color" of the digital coins and see all incoming transactions as standard transactions. For this reason, the added information (metadata) must be verified by those who use colored coins.

The largest US stock exchange platform, NASDAQ[11] used colored coins in their LINQ platform in December 2015. The colored coins were exchanged between private investors and/or banks and linked to securities. LINQ offers a service for secure private transactions and through blockchain technology allows an overview of all previous owners.

After the development of the ERC-20 token standards[12] in November 2015, several colored coin projects on the basis of Bitcoin have either been discontinued or migrated to the Ethereum system (ERC-20 tokens).

With the Segwit update, the Bitcoin system has gained flexibility and is thus able to offer a good basis for future projects in the area of colored coins.

The so-called RGB project is based on the idea of colored coins in conjunction with the Bitcoin Lightning Network and a client-side validation model [98]. This allows a decentralized value transfer with a minimal verification time, a high transaction rate per second and low fees.

---

[11]NASDAQ – National Association of Securities Dealers Automated Quotations.

[12]This is basically a standard for the creation of new digital values based on Ethereum. These are not Ether colored coins, but stand-alone tokens to which any value can be assigned. Further information on this topic can be found at [45, 129, 153].

5.1.2 *Account-Based Solution and Smart Contracts*

The limited and inflexible scripting language of the Bitcoin system motivated developers to create the Ethereum system in 2014. Originally, the Ethereum system was planned as an improved version of a cryptocurrency. It should provide an alternative to the Bitcoin colored coins method[13] and offer a flexible scripting language for the simple development of new functionalities based on an existing blockchain. Ultimately, the Ethereum protocol goes far beyond being a pure currency and offers a blockchain system with a built-in programming language. This makes it possible for everyone to create smart contracts and decentralized applications (dApps) based on their own arbitrary rules for ownership as well as transaction and state transition formats [127].

Ethereum smart contract are far more than mere cryptographic "boxes" with specific values that can only be unlocked if certain conditions are met. They can better be described as "autonomous agents" that exist within the Ethereum system. They have "accounts" as users do and "account numbers" – more specifically addresses. These "autonomous agents" have control over their own contents,[14] for example over the values they contain, conditions, and the Ether balance that can be used for system-dependent fees. Smart contracts always execute a certain part of their source code if they are "triggered" by a special message from another smart contract or a user through a transaction. These "autonomous agents" are executed at the computer of every Ethereum user in a specially created environment: the Ethereum Virtual Machine (EVM) [127].

As a simple example, if a potential tenant has paid the fee for a rental apartment and the day to start the rental has arrived, the smart contract enables a digital key to be sent to the tenant to unlock the apartment [81]. A further well-known example for the use of the smart contract is renting a car or buying one on credit. Based on the general conditions described in the smart contract, the car can be made available to the renter or buyer. If the buyer does not pay a loan installment on time or if the rental period of the car has expired, the car can be blocked for the user.

A connection to information outside the blockchain is enabled for smart contracts through so-called oracles. Oracles function as a bridge to the real world [80]. For example, to convert from US dollars to BTC, an oracle is inserted into the smart contract for the exact conversion at the current exchange rate [127]. The London-based company Provable (formerly Oraclize) offers such a service for connecting blockhain-based DApps (Ethereum, Rootstock, R3 Corda, Hyperledger Fabric and

---

[13]A new meaning is assigned to a value from a UTXO-based blockchain.

[14]Thus, every account in the Ethereum system consists of four fields: nonce, Ether balance, source code and internal storage. A nonce is a transaction counter, and it ensures that each transaction is only executed once. The two last fields are empty in a external account – a user account. Every time the smart contract account is "addressed" by a message or a transaction, its source code is activated. This allows the smart contract to access the internal storage (to read and to write), to send messages to other smart contracts or to create new smart contracts [127].

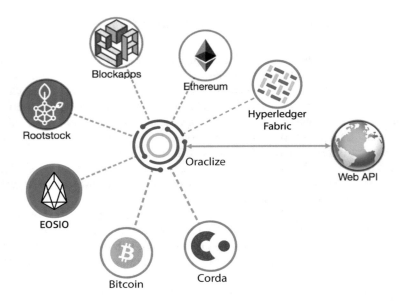

Fig. 5.2 Provable (formerly Oraclize) – Data messenger for decentralized applications [164]

EOS) with any external interfaces of various web applications (Fig. 5.2). One of the Provable projects was Proof-of-Identity [160]. An Ethereum address was thereby linked to an Estonian digital identification number (Digi-ID).

The concept of smart contracts existed long before the development of blockchain technology. Already in 1997, Nick Szabo coined the term "smart contract" in his work "Formalizing and Securing Relationships on Public Networks" [34]. He describes smart contracts as a way to make relationships/ interactions executed via public networks, such as the Internet, secure and legally binding. Smart contracts, according to Szabo, use protocols and user interfaces to facilitate all steps of the contractual process and to reduce costs, when compared to paper-based procedures. Unfortunately, there was no secure replicated database system corresponding to the idea at the time, and thus Nick Szabo's protocol was never put into practice [127].

The challenges of today's smart contracts lie in their legally binding nature as well as in issues of liability and data protection. Who bears the responsibility if an error has crept into the code of a smart contract? Or, how can the legally binding nature of a smart contract be proven in the real world?

The Ethereum hard fork of July 20, 2016 presents an example of what can go wrong. A month earlier 3.6 million Ether (65 million euros) were stolen by an attacker who found a bug in the framework of The DAO. "The DAO" is an application that was implemented as a smart contract on the Ethereum blockchain [178]. The application had no central management institution and was based on rules laid out in the code – for all intents and purposes, a company without its own employees. "The DAO" was, broadly speaking, an investment company that operated crowdfunding through a voting process. After the attack, the Ethereum developers tracked down the bug and decided on a hard fork update in order to get back the stolen Ether. "The DAO" was discontinued after this incident.

In summary, while an account-based solution such as Ethereum offers more flexibility in the creation of new applications by using smart contracts, due to its complexity it is not as robust as the UTXO-based Bitcoin system.

5.1.3   Interoperable Blockchains

Another possibility to securely test or use other blockchains is provided by "interaction between blockchains." In this case, there are both technical (each alt chain[15] implements the technology in its own way) and economical (fluctuating value of the token to be exchanged) challenges.

The authors of the scientific work "Enabling Blockchain Innovations with Pegged Sidechains" [46] describe a new mechanism to enable this interaction. With the help of this mechanism, the tokens/values (hereinafter only "values") of a blockchain can be transferred to another blockchain – the side chain. A sidechain is a blockchain that can recognize and validate data from other blockchains [46].

The idea of a cross blockchain[16] transmission already existed in the past. The procedure,[17] known as an atomic swap or atomic exchange, was already discussed by blockchain developers in 2012, and in 2013 further developed by Tier Nolan (see Appendix E).

In 2014, Adam Back [46] introduced sidechain technology. The core idea here is so-called pegged sidechains. In contrast to a sidechain, a pegged sidechain can transmit back the data received from another blockchain. This mechanism is called a two-way peg and enables blockchain values to be transferred between sidechains in both directions – at a fixed exchange rate. Thus, the user can test a new blockchain by "converting" the existing values, without directly acquiring new blockchain values.

The two-way peg mechanism is available in two versions:

- symmetrical and
- asymmetrical.

---

[15]A separate and independent blockchain that is not built on an already existing blockchain (e.g., Bitcoin) is called an alternative chain, or alt chain for short.

[16]Cross-chain or inter-chain.

[17]Contracts were used for this with a secret exchange and lock-time parameter.

The difference lies in transaction verification. The symmetrical two-way peg mechanism supports SPV,[18] which means verification at both blockchains – parent chain[19] and sidechain – consequently, both blockchains "know" each other. In the asymmetrical procedure, the SPV verification is only done at the parent chain. In this way, the parent chain does not "know" the sidechain and must carry out an SPV verification of the sidechain data, whereby the users of the sidechain can fully examine the parent chain and do not need SPV proof for the parent chain data.

Let's look an example. Alice has bitcoins and would like to have another cryptocurrency or specific values from another blockchain (in our example, the sidechain). She uses the symmetrical procedure for this. She creates a transaction whose output contains a specific address in her parent chain (in this case the Bitcoin blockchain), where her bitcoins are initially blocked for a confirmation period.[20] After the confirmation period has expired, a transaction is created on the sidechain that relates to the output from the Bitcoin blockchain and supports SPV proof. The bitcoins are converted into sidechain values using a fixed exchange rate. Then the values will be blocked for a further one to two days in the sidechain – the so-called contest period. This should prevent the double spending of values. After the contest period is over, Alice has the sidechain values at her disposal (See Fig. 5.3). These values contain information about their parent chain (Bitcoin) and can thus be transferred back in the same way (also with blocked output, confirmation and contest period and SPV proof).

An important factor in the transfer of blockchain values between the sidechains is security. The receiver chain must be able to recognize that the values in the transmitter chain are correctly blocked.

Generally speaking, every blockchain can be adapted to interact with sidechains. The blockchain values can be transmitted between multiple sidechains and back to the parent chain.

The disadvantages of the sidechain technology have been described by its developers as:

- Complexity,
- Risk of fraudulent transmission,
- Risk of the centralization of mining and
- Risk of a soft fork (every change to an existing system can lead to security problems) [46].

---

[18]SPV – Simplified Payment Verification Proof; this gives users the possibility to verify transactions without downloading the entire blockchain (e.g. using block headers).

[19]Parent blockchain.

[20]Confirmation period: 1-2 days.

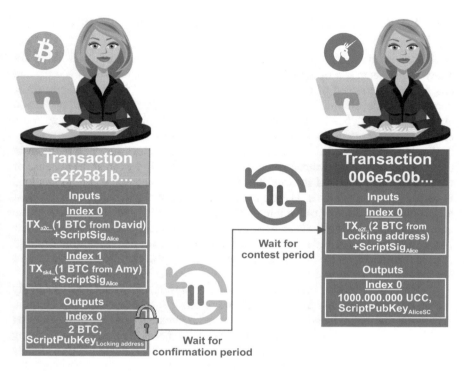

Fig. 5.3 Conversion of bitcoins to sidechain units

The authors of the sidechain article founded the Blockstream company in the year of the article's publication. Their objective was to advance the technology and develop sidechains for various projects.

A project began in 2015 called Rootstock[21] uses the sidechain technology and thereby offers a platform for smart contracts. The Rootstock sidechain has a two-way peg connection to the Bitcoin parent chain, it has no cryptocurrency of its own, and passes on the transaction fees for merged mining[22] to Bitcoin miners. The blocks on the Rootstock sidechain are created every ten seconds.

---

[21] White Paper [20].

[22] Generally, the option exists of either having one's own miners or operating merged mining. Within the realm of merged mining, the process is operated by a blockchain miner for multiple systems at the same time [100]. This means that miners of a blockchain create blocks for several other blockchains. For example, the blocks of the Namecoin blockchain are built by the Bitcoin miners. Each blockchain has its own level of difficulty.

5.2   Implementation of a New, Unique Blockchain Solution

If after an analysis of your needs you decide on your own blockchain, there are many implementation options available. In recent years numerous consortia and projects have emerged that offer "Blockchain-as-a-Service."[23] They support other companies in developing, testing, and providing applications. Multiple application areas have already been conquered by blockchain technology and more and more companies offer ready-made solutions that are tailored to specific areas.

The development of a new blockchain offers greater flexibility and freedom in the composition of the desired functionalities and rules, however, at the expense of the development time and security, since changes to the existing solutions can lead to security gaps and defects. These can be used, for example, in so-called 51 percent attacks, in which a miner or a mining pool has accessibility to more than half of the entire computing capacity (hash rate) in the network and can therefore create new blocks and manipulate them. How vulnerability in the code can be exploited is also seen in the attacks on the decentralized autonomous network "The DAO," which in the meantime has ceased to exist.

As the source code of many blockchain-based systems is public, one can freely use it for their own blockchain applications and adapt it accordingly. Bitcoin, Ethereum, and Hyperledger systems have to a large extent asserted themselves on the blockchain scene. Their source code currently serves as the foundation for many other solutions. A separate and independent blockchain that is not built on an already existing blockchain (e.g., Bitcoin) is called an alternative chain, or alt chain for short.

For a better ideas of which applications are possible based on blockchain technology, or which areas could benefit from this technology, we will take a closer look in the next chapter at existing blockchain projects.

---

[23] A private blockchain is often used for this.

Chapter 6
Projects and Application Areas
of Blockchain Technology

Abstract For a better idea of which applications are possible based on blockchain technology, or which areas can profit from this technology, we will look at already existing blockchain projects. We ask you to note that the projects or companies mentioned in this chapter serve only to illustrate ideas and possible implementations.

It's amazing how fast blockchain technology has spread in a decade. Through numerous projects and intensive research, blockchain technology has undergone rapid development from the original application area of a cryptocurrency, or a decentralized register, to a programmable decentralized trust infrastructure. Currently, there is hardly any area of application with a decentralized infrastructure in which the introduction of blockchain has not been attempted. Science, medicine (for more on the subject of blockchain and medicine, see the book by E. Boettinger and J. zu Putlitz "Die Zukunft der Medizin"(The Future of Medicine), the chapter "Die Zukunftspotenziale der Blockchain-Technologie" (The Future Potential of Blockchain Technology) [24]), identity management, cloud computing, cloud storage, the Internet of Things, finance, insurance, logistics, retail, energy supply – these and other sectors are the beneficiaries of blockchain. Numerous startups were founded that offer blockchain as the total solution or as part of the solution. They either use an existing blockchain (e.g., Bitcoin or Ethereum) or develop their own. Also companies with a developed infrastructure and established products and services, such as IBM, Microsoft, Samsung, SAP, Intel and many others, have been working with this technology for a long time and are starting new projects in this area.

Naturally, we must also remember that not every new blockchain project has been crowned with success. We've chosen not to provide any figures here since statistics often include pseudo-blockchain projects. Therefore the hype surrounding blockchain technology is not only a driver of development, but, at the same time, the main reason for numerous failures. The planning and development phases of many projects that depend on trend technologies are often extremely accelerated. This is done with the intention of getting the product on the market as quickly as possible and benefiting from the hype. With such an approach, negligence in understanding the technology and the essential role of security often have a pivotal effect on the outcome. It is therefore advisable to either address the problem and look for an appropriate technology or at least to first deal with the technology and be able to take advantage of its strengths.

Whether we use an UTXO or an account-based model does not initially depend on the area of application of the blockchain technology but on the specific problem. It is thereby necessary to take into account the focal points and characteristics of the respective model in relation to your concept.

By looking at the following use cases, We can summarize the advantages of a system made up of numerous participants who trust neither the other participants nor the other intermediaries and want to interact with the system:

- Tracking possession of a value.

  For example, when buying and selling paintings at auctions it is easy to prove the origin, previous owner and current owner (when, where, by whom?).
- Joint control over specific values (Multi-Signature).
- Voting.

  FollowMyVote offers in collaboration with BitShares a voting platform based on blockchain. The system protects votes by ensuring that they will not be altered by third parties, as well as offering transparency and flexibility.
- Automated contracts.

  For booking and renting private accommodations as well as cars and bicycles, among other things.
- Games, including gambling.
- Identity and reputation systems.

  Since more and more health data is being generated through new technology, (for example, wearable devices like fitness wristbands or smart watches) the need for this data to be stored securely and digitally cannot be underestimated – also with limited access granted to specific data. In healthcare, a smart profile can also give patients the ability to decide for themselves about whether to share their own data. Furthermore, it is possible using the blockchain, for example, to share this anonymized data with researchers (Public Research Repository), learn more about one's own illness, communicate with others who share the illness, carry out fundraising or crowdfunding, and keep track of digital prescriptions and invoices [95]. At the blockchain technology conference "Consensus 2017," in New York in May 2017, the Los Angeles-based startup company "Gem" presented the first blockchain product for health data management (Fig. 6.1) [124].
- Decentralized markets.

  For example, OpenBazaar uses blockchain technology for P2P online trading. Users can act as buyers or sellers and pay for purchased goods in bitcoins, Bitcoin Cash, Litecoin or Zcash. The sale and purchase are secured by a 2-of-3 multi-signature smart contract. When the buyer and seller agree on the product and price, the buyer sends the money to the smart contract address. If the deal is successful, and the buyer and seller are both satisfied, the buyer releases the

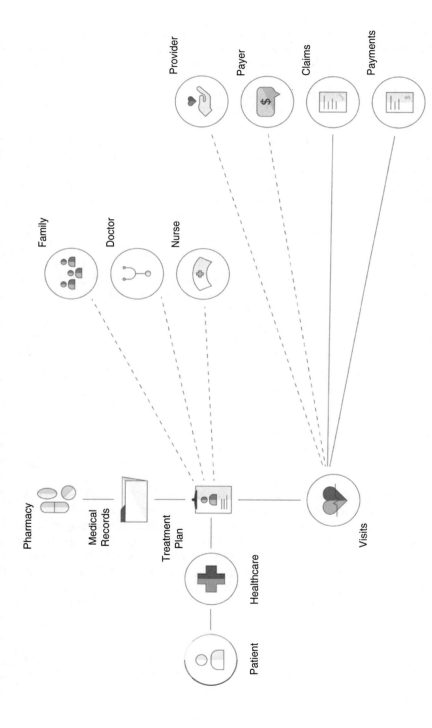

Fig. 6.1 Gem – The blockchain for health data [124]

money to the seller (both sign the payout transaction of the multi-signature address). If one of the two business partners is dissatisfied (e.g., the goods are not delivered or the buyer did not pay for them), a moderator intervenes in the communication. The moderator has the third private key for the multi-signature address [158, 159].

- Decentralized data storage or data processing.

  One reader or another would likely argue that this area mainly involves efficiency, and that providers with centrally managed solutions are far superior to blockchain solutions with their current limitations in scalability. In fact, today there exists a huge amount of cloud solutions (cloud storage and cloud computing), with market leaders "giants" like Amazon, Microsoft, IBM and Google [110]. Users often pay for such solutions with their data. A P2P cloud solution thus arose that is independent of a central instance, and in which the users of the system make their resources (storage or computing resources) available to other users and are rewarded for this. Many providers have already partially implemented this idea. For example, with the cloud storage solutions, the files to be stored are first encrypted, and then split into smaller fragments, and first then are these fragments distributed to the users who have made their storage resources available. The information where, for example, the individual fragments (so-called metadata) are saved is often centrally stored.[1] Some providers also strive to offer a decentralized solution for the metadata and leave the decision up to the users whether they store their metadata locally or externally at a cloud storage provider of their choice (Storj is an example of this [180, 181]). The blockchain technology, specifically Blockchain 2.0, offers numerous advantages with such a solution. For example, the administrative layer (where and how the fragments of the files are to be stored and who and to what extent is to be rewarded, etc.) can be decentralized with the help of such solutions.

- Decentralized autonomous organizations.

  As we have already seen, so-called decentralized autonomous organizations (DAOs) are possible through blockchain technology. This means that the organization has neither a business manager, nor any other central leadership instance or company headquarters, but instead has a decentralized structure with automated decision-making according to defined rules. These rules are determined by the majority decisions of the involved participants and continuously developed [101]. DAOs buy products and services in compliance with their smart contracts from third parties, who are so-called contractors. Payment is made in cryptocurrency. Based on the specifications, the contractors produce their products and services, which are in turn are used or marketed by the DAO. Through the marketing of these products and services the DAO earns money that is reinvested or can

---

[1] A good example of this is the Bdrive solution [48] from the Bundesdruckerei, with the difference that the encrypted and authenticated data fragments are not distributed to users, but are distributed to independent cloud storage services that are ISO-certified and whose data centers are operated in Germany [49].

be divided among its shareholders [149]. The first decentralized autonomous organization was called "The DAO" and existed for less than a year. It could be manipulated due to a bug in its code. After several software updates, which were intended to fix the bug and the consequences of the attack, "The DAO" was discontinued [127].

Social networks and the free press also benefit from blockchain technology. Steemit is a blockchain-based social media platform. The users of the platform publish their content (e.g., news) and are rewarded by other users in their own cryptocurrency [179]. Karma, All.me, and Minds are just a few of the many blockchain-based projects in the field of social networks.

Another blockchain solution is not only aimed at a specific target group but sees itself as a layer of people in a technical architecture (in a decentralized protocol stack). The Colony protocol is a Ethereum smart contract that allows developers to integrate into their applications decentralized and self-regulating work scheduling, decision-making and financial management. This means that thanks to the Colony solution, pseudonymous and decentralized organizations can be created, whose employees come from all over the world and digitally join together for one or more projects and are rewarded for their engagement [96].

The company Peerism, on the other hand, concentrates on the skills and abilities of individual people, adding these to so-called skill tokens. It aims to bring people together with paid jobs/assignments.

When compared internationally, the greatest concentration of blockchain companies are in the US and China, followed by Great Britain, Singapore and South Korea [91].

The topic of blockchain is not only being pursued by individual companies; rather, several countries are devoting themselves to the topic at the national level. In Germany, on June 29, 2017, a blockchain federation based in Berlin was founded. It has more than 20 working groups and published a position paper in October of the same year with recommendations for making Germany a global player in the worldwide blockchain ecosystem [87].

Two years later, in September 2019, the Federal Government of Germany launched a comprehensive blockchain strategy. This strategy is intended to contribute to the digital sovereignty and competitive ability of Germany and Europe and to support the digital transformation already initiated in the country. Particular attention is thereby paid to the creation of an investment and growth-oriented regulatory framework for the development and use of blockchain technology. The strategy provides for various measures to initially examine the "suitability" of blockchain technology. For example, the topic will be integrated into ongoing initiatives for digital transformation; living labs and a round table on blockchain will be created, and a call for tenders launched for numerous studies.

These measures are planned to take the form of these five fields of action:

• Ensuring stability and stimulating innovation. Through the creation of clear and stable statutory and legal frameworks, the Federal Government wants to encourage investments in digital technologies and to maintain the stability of the financial system. The Federal Government will publish a bill to regulate the public offering of certain crypto-tokens. Before the publication of the offer, the crypto-token providers must first provide an information sheet created by the Federal Financial Supervisory Authority (BaFin) in accordance with the legal requirements, which must then be published. At the same time, those who offer custody services for cryptocurrency or any services in connection with special crypto values are also subject to money laundering regulations. Service providers in Germany who offer the exchange of cryptocurrencies into other cryptocurrencies and cryptocurrencies into fiat currencies already require permission from the BaFin. They also obligated to comply with the money laundering laws. The Federal Government also wants to ensure the stability of the financial system by avoiding the so-called stablecoins.[2] It seeks to work at the European and international level to ensure that these coins do not become an alternative to federal currencies [89].

- Bringing innovation to maturity. To this end, projects and living labs from specific application areas are promoted: namely, energy, law, logistics, production, verification of higher education certification, and consumer protection. A concrete measure in the energy sector is the piloting of a blockchain-based energy systems connection by the Federal Government. In the legal sector, the Federal Government supports an "Industry 4.0 – Legal Testbed." A test environment for the development of secure digital business processes is being established for this. The focus is on legal questions about smart contracts in machine-to-machine communication. The test environment is initially planned for logistics and production. With another funding measure, "Industry 4.0 – Collaboration in Dynamic Value-Added Networks," the Federal Government seeks to research if and how the use of blockchain technology can contribute to transparency in supply and value chains. Here, emphasis is placed on company cooperations (smart contracts) and process data transmission. The employment of blockchain solutions for verifying the proof of competency (certificates, ECTS) initially in the areas of international student mobility and vocational diplomas and continuing education certificates will be checked and in specific cases funded by the Federal Government. The Federal Government also plans to use properties of blockchain technology, such as transparency and decentralization, in the area of consumer protection. With this in mind, the Federal Government will develop and promote blockchain applications that contribute to consumer protection, for example, in the food chain [89].
- Enabling investments. The Federal Government seeks to offer companies and organizations sufficient investment security for the use of blockchain technology by setting up clear framework conditions (development of standards, possibility of certification and compliance with IT security requirements). The Federal

---

[2]Stablecoins, as the name suggests, are cryptocurrencies with low volatility, i.e., stable prices, measured in fiat currency. This is achieved by coupling the cryptocurrency with a good that has a stable value (e.g., gold or a fiat currency such as the euro) [68].

Government is therefore planning to investigate the possibilities for introducing accredited certification procedures that can be used by manufacturers and providers on a volunteer basis. Among other things, the Federal Government would like to investigate the enforceability of law in blockchain structures. For example, whether blockchain technology can be implemented in the area of evidence verification,[3] or for the management of copyright protected contents.[4] The Federal Government also plans to focus on the legal framework for decentralized autonomous organizations (DAO) and supports the development of such digital innovations. The Federal Government will further address other legal issues and investigate the potential of blockchain technology for an international arbitration board and for the identification of natural or legal persons in the regulatory system. The Federal Government seeks to become involved in the development of standards at an international level and act as an advocate for the use of open interfaces [89].

- Applying technology. The full title for this point is: "Applying technology: digitized administrative services." This category will, however, likely disappoint the reader since the content hardly reflects the title. Few specific projects are being launched that could demonstrate the intention of a well thought-out digitization strategy for an administrative infrastructure. Further approaches and possibilities of blockchain technology are being examined and tested and the topic integrated into existing digitization initiatives. Specifically, the Federal Government is focusing in this area on blockchain-based digital identities – so-called "Self-Sovereign Identities" (more on the topic of "Self-Sovereign Identities" in Sect. 6.2). This means, they will check whether this solution promises benefits when compared to existing solutions. The blockchain strategy of the Federal Government is based on information gathered from online consultation with numerous companies and organizations. This consultation resulted in a divided opinion regarding a state-owned infrastructure for blockchain applications that is intended to support companies and organizations in developing specific applications. Opponents of this idea do not see the state as the appropriate actor for building a blockchain infrastructure. Thus, the infrastructural activities of the state are bound with the hope of establishing standards for interoperability and governance structures for decentralized networks. Taking a less than ideal position, the Federal Government hopes that the municipalities will pioneer the set up of the first blockchain infrastructures and thereby lay the foundation for blockchain technology in implementing administrative services. This contradicts the wish for interoperability and a comprehensive blockchain infrastructure. The Federal Government is instead involved in setting up the European blockchain services infrastructure (EBSI). This initiative is driven by the European Blockchain Partnership in which Germany is a member. The first

---

[3]How data from a blockchain can be sent to courts of law or any verification authorities [89].

[4]For example, for complex works with many contributors, such as those in the film or music industries [89].

use cases include the exchange of certificates and a blockchain-based register of the European Court of Auditors (ECA). The Federal Government strives to continue its public promotion of lighthouse projects on the subject of blockchain technology in administration. The Federal Government is also planning on investigating the deployment of blockchain technology in the following use cases: any application cases in connection with administrative services that offer an alternative to the written form and personal appearance; the assignment of digital validity tokens to certificates and public documents for their digital verification; blockchain-based applications for more efficient and transparent customs valuation of e-commerce transactions in third countries; the linking of systems with each other containing vehicle data, in particular with regard to the administration of powers of disposal for motor vehicles [89].

- Disseminating information. According to online-consultation [90] 43 percent of the surveyed decision-makers from medium-sized German companies stated in an online survey from the Federal Statistical Office (2017) that they were not aware of any possible uses for blockchain. On the other hand, eighteen percent of those surveyed stated that they knew that the blockchain technology could be used to manage certificates of authenticity. In the online consultation [90], the Federal Government confirms that in spite of the widespread dissemination of blockchain technology, there is a large gap in blockchain knowledge regarding what is known inside the blockchain community and that which is known by mid-sized company leadership and the general population. The Federal Government thus plans to greatly increase its support of the number of new, open forms of cooperation between companies, as well as actors in civil society and scientific institutions. According to the Federal Government, especially among SMEs (small and medium-sized enterprises) there are complex use cases in which blockchain technology could be implemented to great benefit. Therefore, in the context of the existing initiatives (Digital Hub Initiative and Mittelstand 4.0 competence centers), the government supports the exchange between SMEs, start-ups, large companies, and other relevant organizations. The Federal Government sees the particular importance of blockchain technology in the legally secure access it offers to data and its re-use, in particular, in the energy sector (data of producers and consumers for research, business, and society). Thus, the Federal Government is examining whether the GDPR is compliant and plans a pilot project to test a data platform that visualizes the origin and concentration of CO_2 in an urban area [89].

The Federal Government has announced that it will check the blockchain strategy regularly and develop it further. In the appendix of the strategy, a table of actions can be found where the individual actions are listed with the corresponding responsible persons. Unfortunately, this table is of little use without time specifications.

In Europe, Estland is among the pioneers in the area of blockchain and calls itself "e-Estonia." The Estonian cabinet has already been working paperless since 1999 [41] (see Fig. 6.2), and the Estonian government experimenting with blockchain since its emergence in 2008. According to its own statements [106], since 2012 the

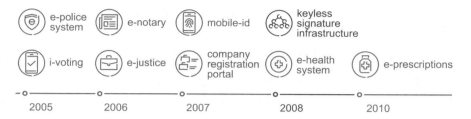

Fig. 6.2 Estonia's path of digitization [106]

blockchain has been introduced in many registers in Estonia, such as in health care, and in parliamentary, judicial and security sectors. Estonia uses a KSI blockchain that was developed by the Estonian company Guardtime [107, 136]. This technology is also used by NATO, the US Department of defense, and the EU Information System for Cybersecurity [106]. It can be argued whether the blockchain definition in the context of the KSI blockchain is a private permissioned blockchain or a technology that uses cryptographic hash functions to link data/information with each other (linked timestamping) [136].

Among other, Sweden has also expressed interest in blockchain technology. A blockchain-based[5] register has existed there since 2017 [85]. The Netherlands welcomes the opportunity to play a leading role internationally in the blockchain technology sector. In March 2017, the national coalition of blockchain technology in the Netherlands (Dutch Blockchain Coalition[6]) presented a comprehensive action plan to the Dutch Ministry of Economic Affairs [94, 105]. After numerous studies on the possibilities of blockchain technology in 2019/2020, with the pre-selected application cases ("Self-Sovereign Identities",[7] logistics, academic certificates and diplomas, etc.), the DBC aims to become involved in practical application [105].

A detailed overview of the blockchain projects in Europe is provided by the "European Union Blockchain Observatory and Forum." This is an initiative of the European Commission [122].

In the following, some of the applications and projects in which blockchain technology is already being used are explained in greater detail.

6.1 Financial Sector

The financial sector is the very first area where blockchain technology has found growing application. While a large number of cryptocurrencies have been introduced since the inception of Bitcoin, not all of them have prevailed. The currently

---

[5]Private Blockchain.

[6]DBC is a Dutch joint venture between partners from government, science and industry [105].

[7]More on the subject of "Self-Sovereign Identity" in Sect. 6.2.

well-known and widespread cryptocurrencies besides bitcoin (market capitalization approx. 158 billion euros[8]) are:

- XRP from Ripple (market capitalization approx. EUR 8 billion[9]),
- Litecoin (market capitalization approx. EUR 3 billion[10]),
- XMR from Monero (market capitalization approx. EUR 1 billion[11]),
- Dash (market capitalization approx. EUR 700 million[12]).

The US company Ripple has been active in the financial sector since 2013 and offers banks a blockchain-based[13] real-time money transfer service as well as supporting different fiat[14]- and cryptocurrencies.

Besides the stock exchange company NASDAQ[15] in the US and ASX[16] in Australia, numerous financial companies are already using blockchain technology. Many blockchain consortia have sprung up in different areas, including those in the financial sector whose members are finance companies. The Japanese blockchain consortium BCCC already numbers over 200 members [47]. The blockchain consortium R3, based in New York, has over 300 members [165]. Many banks (e.g. Deutsche Bank, Santander, Commerzbank, etc.) are currently experimenting with the technology [152].

The majority of these financial service companies are interested in using blockchain technology to organize the exchange of transactions with each other (e.g. the possibility of joint management of KYC data[17]). Some of them also use blockchain technology in the solutions they offer their customers (e.g., securities processing). Blockchain solutions in the financial sector are primarily applications that use smart contracts, for example the blockchain promissory note used by Daimler AG and the Landesbank Baden-Württemberg (LBBW) [103].

In addition to the major players in the financial industry, numerous start-ups were founded that offer blockchain solutions to other companies in the area of finance. For example, the blockchain company Clearmatics, founded in 2015 and based in London, promotes the development of the decentralized financial market infrastructure (dFMI). The goal is to create a broader ecosystem for value

---

[8]May 2020.

[9]May 2020.

[10]May 2020.

[11]May 2020.

[12]May 2020.

[13]Private blockchain.

[14]Fiat currency or fiat money is money that is not covered by assets. It is used as a medium of exchange but has no intrinsic value. Today's currency systems are usually not covered by a commodity. For example, money issued by a central bank such as the euro or dollar is called fiat money.

[15]NASDAQ – National Association of Securities Dealers Automated Quotations.

[16]ASX is the Australian securities exchange located in Sydney.

[17]Know Your Customer.

transfer, which is cryptographically secure and that functions without financial intermediaries. Clearmatics works with the Ethereum Foundation and is an active member of the Ethereum Enterprise Alliance (EEA) [93].

6.2   Identity Management

The topic of identity management[18] is undoubtedly one that most of us have already encountered privately and/or professionally, as are the challenges that go along with it. We are asked again and again to disclose our personal data (name, address, telephone number, credit card number, etc.), to make it available upon logging in to every new online service, and to trust that it will be stored safely. In addition, there are huge amounts of login data that we must keep and manage ourselves securely. From the user's point of view, it would make much more sense to assign different services partial authorization for certain digital identity data than to create a new identity for each new service.

Of course there are also many solutions on the market for this problem. In addition to being user-friendly, they must be able to guarantee a secure infrastructure. Solutions that lay the foundation for a so-called user-centric identity,[19] such as the OpenID method or OpenID Connect, allow users to log in (authenticate and authorize) to various online services, as long as they are supported [43].

Having an interoperable digital identity, whose release for other services requires the consent of the user, still does not mean that the user has complete control over his personal date. A so-called self-sovereign identity (SSI) goes beyond the user-centric identity and allows the user to remain in control of his own data, to decide who is allowed to have access to what personal data, for how long, with whom the data can be shared, etc. This precedes the creation of a decentralized trust infrastructure, which allows the user to make identity statements (regarding his address, ownership of a valid driver's license, credit standing, membership in a chess club, a degree certificate, retirement, etc.) that are certified and verified – so-called claims (see Fig. 6.3) [43].

The ideas and principles of a self-sovereign identity (SSI) are well-defined and described in the work of Christopher Allen, "The Path to Self-Sovereign

---

[18]Digital identities, also called electronic identities, include all operations in which people, objects and processes authenticate themselves online via certain attributes to prove their own identity. A digital identity can be clearly assigned to the person, the object or the process in question. Digital identities come in a great variety of forms: the simplest way to authenticate oneself in an online account is to log in with the user name and password. Companies often use employee ID cards to allow their employees access to the company premises or to provide them access to special information [88].

[19]The user-centered design turned centralized identities into interoperable federated identities with centralized control, while maintaining a certain level of user consent as to how and with whom the user's digital identity is shared [43].

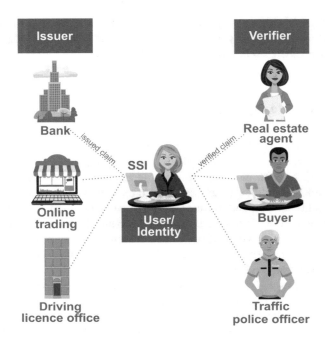

Fig. 6.3 Self-Sovereign Identity (SSI)

Identity." At this time, several standards for the implementation of SSIs have been developed. The two best known foundations for a SSI that have become standards are DID (Decentralized Identifier[20]) and "verifiable credentials" from W3C.[21] Other standards are DID Auth and DKMS (Decentralized Key Management System [198]). This allows thousands of DIDs to be created for an SSI, each of which can establish a life-long, encrypted, trusted channel with another person, an organization or object. DIDs as well as SSI make central registries obsolete and are based on a decentralized infrastructure [43, 177]. Numerous SSI projects use public or private blockchains for this. Others see more potential for a self-sovereign identity in the so-called Distributed Ledger Technology (DLT).

Various online service providers adapt the DID standard for their own solution and develop their own DID methods[22] (see Fig. 6.4). These are published and summarized in a W3C register [195].

---

[20]DIDs are URLs that link a DID subject to a DID document. DIDs documents are simple documents that describe how the DID can be used, for example what verification methods must be implemented [193].

[21]W3C – World Wide Web Consortium is an international community that is involved with the development of standards for the World Wide Web [194].

[22]A DID method defines the manner in which a DID and the corresponding DID document from a blockchain or DLT are read and written [177].

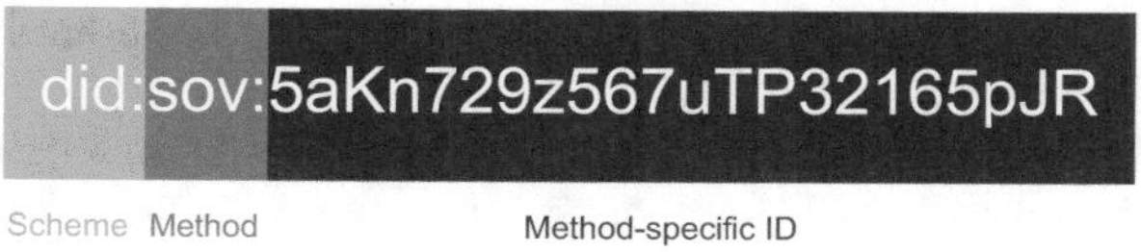

Fig. 6.4 An example of DID
Syntax (W3C) [195–197]

did:sov:5aKn729z567uTP32165pJR

Scheme Method   Method-specific ID

Already various SSI providers have entered their own methods in the register, such as Sovrin [175], SelfKey [169], uPort [187] and Jolocom [145]. Blockstack has also published its DID method in the register. Currently, the blockchain identity provider Blockstack offers a decentralized computing platform for the development of secure applications that gives back to users control over their data and identity [82, 83].

On November 15, 2018, the Federal Blockchain Association (the Blockchain Bundesverband) also published a comprehensive statement on the subject of self-sovereign identity. This serves as a call to action in business and politics and contributes to a global, universal identity framework [75, 76].

6.3 Internet of Things

In addition to people, objects and processes also have digital identities. In the area of the Internet of Things – IoT – every device has its own digital image that identifies it uniquely in a network, thereby enabling interaction with other devices and people. The IoT devices are as a rule miniaturized computers that have diverse sensors, low storage and computing resources as well as a limited energy supply. They are usually connected to a powerful IoT hub, also called a gateway. The gateway enables the IoT device to then be connected to the cloud, from which they are controlled. "Smart" devices thus lacks autonomy. Additionally, the individual IoT systems use different cloud infrastructures, which makes comprehensive P2P communication difficult [182].

Blockchain technology makes autonomy and interoperability for P2P communication possible without intermediaries and a central authority. IoT devices can, for example, have their own Ethereum accounts controlled by smart contracts or they can generate smart contracts themselves. A challenge is created by the limited resources of IoT devices. It is already problematic for most devices to run an application for lightweight users (lightweight nodes, as described in Sect. 3.2).

The German company Slock.it offers a solution for this situation in the form of a net service client. The net service client is a part of the so-called INCUBED network.[23] This solution enables the connection of low performance IoT devices

---

[23]Trustless Incentivized Remote Node Network.

to a blockchain[24] without the necessity of extra hardware or significant Internet bandwidth [171–173].

The Slock.it company's first product was an intelligent door lock that could be opened via a smartphone app. Companies like Airbnb can benefit from such a solution in the future. Slock.it currently offers its experience and solutions in three different applications: e-charging mobility,[25] energy[26] and governance[27] [174].

The company Filament also uses blockchain technology in IoT solutions. The emphasis here is on industrial applications of the IoT [143]. With this target in mind, the company has developed its own secure hardware that supports advanced cryptographic functions and is also physically protected. Such Filament solutions can, for example, be deployed to optimize the value and supply chain.

The IBM solution for this application area is called Watson IoT Platform. This service makes it possible to transfer the data sent by IoT devices to a private blockchain [141].

Following a blockchain and IoT summit in December 2016, several well-known, large companies and blockchain startups came together with a common goal.[28] Together they want to lay the foundation for IoT providers to make core functions available for use with different blockchains [170].

A consortium called "Chain of Things" supports collaborative development of open-source standards for blockchain technology in the IoT area. Three projects have already been created on this basis:

- Chain of Security (secure IoT applications),
- Chain of Solar (ElectriCChain Solar Project: Connects IoT and blockchain technology for use in the solar energy sector),
- Chain of Shipping (IoT and blockchain technology in the context of trade, shipping and transport).

The combination of IoT and blockchain technology finds application primarily in the areas of energy and logistics.

---

[24]Chain-agnostic: A single Incubed client can connect to multiple blockchains at the same time [173].

[25]The focus here is on a simple and secure payment method for charging electric cars.

[26]Here, a simplified process for tracing and supplying renewable energy to end users is the focal point.

[27]This application involves a project with Siemens, whereby Siemens employees can vote on social initiatives.

[28]Bosch, Cisco, Gemalto, Foxconn, Ambisafe, BitSE, Chronicled, ConsenSys, Distributed, Filament, Hashed Health, Ledger, Skuchain and Slock.it.

6.4 Energy

Since local producers of renewable energy are also affected as soon as conventional networks fail [137], microgrids[29] are necessary to operate local energy trade. A microgrid in conjunction with blockchain and IoT technology makes it is possible to trade locally produced renewable energy in a local marketplace. For example, one can sell surplus energy generated by roof solar panels (an energy unit becomes a blockchain token) to a neighbor (using smart contracts) without having to rely on a middleman.

The first project to make this idea a reality was Brooklyn Microgrid (BMG), developed and implemented by the company LO3 Energy. The system connects households in the New York district of Brooklyn that own solar energy systems ("prosumer") with households that want to buy local solar energy ("consumers") [84].

The Brooklyn project has provided inspiration for another project in Germany: the Landau Microgrid Project (LAMP). This is a pilot and research project from the Karlsruhe Institute of Technology (KIT) in collaboration with the energy producer Energie Südwest AG and the company LO3 Energy. Blockchain technology is also used in the context of the project for the local trading of electricity products. Twenty households have access to a blockchain-based trading platform. There, locally produced "green" energy can be traded between households. Via an app, participants have access to their own electricity consumption and production data and can specify their price expectations for locally generated energy from renewable sources [148].

Accordingly, approximately 60 percent of all blockchain projects and DLT projects in the energy sector focus on the topic of the P2P microgrid network [97]. Other blockchain solutions also concentrate on energy production trade but in the B2C context (Business-to-Consumer). For example, the solution mentioned in the last chapter from the company Slock.it: an app that enables users to find charging stations for electric cars in their area and to pay easily and securely via the blockchain.

Other blockchain solutions in the energy sector concentrate on the tracking and management of data connected with energy production and use. For example, the project ElectriCChain from the consortium "Chain of Things." The goal of this project is to connect the currently ten million solar energy systems worldwide and to send the real-time data to the blockchain or to a distributed ledger [109]. This should, for example, give scientists the possibility to get an overview of the solar energy generation data and thus to analyze it. The project supports the development of open standards and tools for writing and reading the energy generation data in and from the blockchain or a distributed ledger.

---

[29]A microgrid is an energy network that unites energy producers and consumers in a network or sub-network that can be operated autonomously [202].

6.5   Logistics

Regarding IoT technology, there are several possible use cases in logistics. Highly sensitive goods can, for example, be equipped with IoT devices with the necessary sensors and thus send the information collected to the blockchain. The company Modum.io offers a solution for tracking information pertaining to the storage conditions of medicine (temperature, humidity) along the entire supply chain.

Logistics affects several business areas of a company and generates huge amounts of information that is exchanged between the parties involved in the flow of goods. Today, supply chains are very complex and include numerous participants from all over the world. These participants have varying rights of access to the information and tasks. Thus, a blockchain-based supply chain management can provide the following advantages to a company (see Fig. 6.5):

- Cyptographic verification replaces trust – thus, the possibility of simple access authorization and user management.
- Secure logging of data and transparency of content to guarantee a fail-safe performance, counterfeit protection, and data traceability.
- A decentralized participant network, smart contracts and oracles can replace numerous middlemen. When passing specific destinations in the supply chain, the conditions stored in the smart contracts can be checked and additional tasks/functions activated (for example, the service can be paid for in full if all of the conditions are met).

On August 9, 2018, IBM and Maersk[30] presented their blockchain-based[31] solution for the shipping and logistics industry. It allows an exchange of events and documents in real-time along the entire supply chain with the help of a digital infrastructure. Sustainable transport is supported through the transparency of all processes involved, as well as the provision of secure access to certain data for certain users [142, 185].

Foxconn, one of the world's largest producers of electronics and computer parts developed a blockchain-based supply chain financial platform with the Chinese online lending platform Dianrong. The project will initially focus on the automotive, electronics, and clothing industries. In this way, payments and transactions in the supply chain should become more transparent, manageable, and easier to authenticate. With blockchain technology, efficiency will be increased in the entire supply chain and costs cut with the elimination of third party providers. Not only will the financial flow be processed on the basis of blockchain technology, but the entire supply chain as well. If all the transactions of the supply chain become easier to validate, the efficiency of the entire ecosystem will increase [167].

---

[30]The largest container shipping company worldwide.

[31]Private permissioned blockchain. TradeLens uses the die IBM blockchain platform, which is based on Hyperledger Fabric.

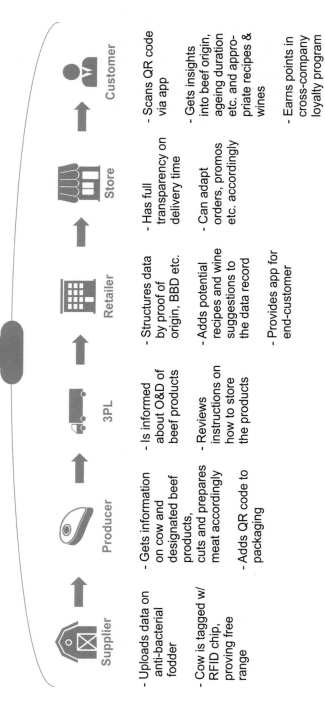

Fig. 6.5 End-to-end blockchain-based supply chain [201]

Another blockchain-based project in the logistics sector called DELIVER targets container logistics. The project came about through a cooperation between the Port Authority of Rotterdam, the Dutch bank ABN Amro, and Samsung SDS (the logistics and IT branch of Samsung). Physical, administrative and financial flows are thereby digitally integrated into the supply chain [155, 162].

Transparent and traceable supply chains are especially important for end customers. Sectors such as pharmacology, and the textile and food industries could in this way re-establish consumer confidence.

Chapter 7
Summary

Abstract The time has now come to draw conclusions and summarize what has been discussed in previous chapters. We hope we have succeeded in helping you to form your own opinion about blockchain technology. In combining the information provided here with your own experience, it is our hopeful intention that you will be in a better place to decide what is truly innovative about blockchain technology – and what is little more than hype.

We live in an age of digitization, the benefits of which can be found in all areas of life. Business processes as well as those in daily life have become leaner, faster, more efficient, and more convenient. Today we acknowledge new inventions and innovations without hardly batting an eye. The image of the entrepreneur who keeps business information on a large hard drive and carries it everywhere, or stores it on a laptop and locks it in a company safe, seems absurd and outdated. Data should be quickly and easily accessible from everywhere and stored in such a way as to protect its confidentiality. To do this, we can either use our own hardware and software infrastructure or that of a service provider. The market is full of solutions. On the provider's side we encounter near monopolies: Amazon, Google, Microsoft, Apple, SAP and Facebook divide up the digital market among themselves. For the most part, customers accept this, grateful these tech giants offer interoperable solutions[1] that are readily accepted and widely used in society. Work is continually being done on these solutions, which adds to our sense of security. We thus place our trust and data in centralized solutions and accept the dependency that goes along with it.

In his Bitcoin paper,[2] Satoshi Nakamoto wrote that commerce on the Internet is almost exclusively dependent on financial institutions who act as trusted third parties for the processing of electronic payment transactions. Further, there is no mechanism that allows for payment processing via a communications channel and without a trusted entity. It was just this situation that created the demand for an electronic payment system that could replace trust with cryptographic proof and

---

[1] In the context of the respective provider, such as the interoperability of solutions from Apple.

[2] Bitcoin: A Peer-to-Peer Electronic Cash System [26].

© Springer Nature Switzerland AG 2021
T. Gayvoronskaya, C. Meinel, *Blockchain*,
https://doi.org/10.1007/978-3-030-61559-8_7

allow users to interact directly with each other without a trusted third party. The idea and desire for decentralization – sparked when the Internet first came into being – was rekindled.

In this book we have already described several challenges of decentralized systems in contrast to centralized models. Processes, such as the administration of resources and systems, are distributed to all users in the system. This creates the first challenge: reaching agreement on a state of the system that is "right for everyone."[3] This agreement, or so-called consensus, is made more difficult by the fact that individual system users do not know or trust each other (see Sect. 3.3). In addition, there is the possibility that one or more users could have malicious intentions and try to manipulate the system (see Sect. 4.2).

Historically-speaking, consensus solutions for decentralized systems have been dependent on a number of conditions (permissioned systems). For instance, the number of system users and/or their identities must be known. Solutions such as the Byzantine Agreement (BA) algorithm, or Paxos or Raft are intended for decentralized systems with a limited or static number of users. A majority decision is thereby reached among pre-selected users (so-called master nodes). The robustness of such a system is based on the number of malicious users it can tolerate under real conditions. Despite these conditions, the threat of a Sybil attack remains. In this scenario, the attacker creates many false "identities" in a decentralized system with the intent of manipulating or disturbing the system's communication [70].

The state of the system in blockchain technology as "right/true for everybody" is determined by the "longest chain"[4] (see Sect. 3.3). In other words, the order and execution of contents (transactions, see Sect. 4.1.1) in the longest chain are correct/true based on user votes. Since users vote on the "longest chain" with their computing power (Proof-of-Work – PoW), this also means that ultimately the chain with the most votes contains the most work. The Nakamoto consensus mechanism, which is anchored in blockchain technology, relies on the fact that the majority of computing power in a system without participation conditions (permissionless system) is in the hands of the honest users, and not that the majority of the users are honest. Users are free to join the network or to leave it.

Users are rewarded for their voting effort. They must follow the rules in order to keep losses at a minimum (energy consumption due to an expenditure of computing power) and win the competition to gain the reward. In the Bitcoin system, the competition for the reward has led to hardware "upgrading" by users (miners) who are involved in consensus building. Many miners band together into so-called mining pools to bundle their computing capacity. This results in an ever-increasing rise in energy consumption and the associated costs. The greatest point of criticism in the Proof-of-Work concept is in fact the excessive use of electrical energy.

---

[3]Which order and execution of contents are correct and which are not.

[4]The contents are cryptographically linked to one another in a specific form (see Sects. 4.1.1 and 4.1.2).

Accordingly, some blockchain-based applications rely on alternatives to PoW, such as the Proof-of-Stake concept. In contrast to PoW, the PoS concept is not based on a required amount of computing power but on a proportion of digital coins in a cryptocurrency. A user who owns n percent of the digital coins may create n percent of the blocks. However, the security level of alternatives is far lower than their PoW counterpart (see Sects. 3.3 and 4.2).

We thus come to the next challenge – the scalability trilemma[5] (see Sect. 4.2.2). By attempting to adapt blockchain technology to suit one's own needs and "make it more efficient" either decentralization or the security of the system is lost. In terms of efficiency, a blockchain-based system (PoW-based public blockchain) can therefore not compete with a comparable centralized solution, such as Hyperledger Fabric or Ripple (which use a permissioned blockchain) with thousands of transactions per second [32]. This is not because blockchain technology is still new and unoptimized, but is due to the inherent nature of the technology [32].

For this reason, in developing their public-permissionless blockchain solutions companies choose decentralized and secure solutions and work on optimizing their scalability to fit their needs, as in the case of the best known and most successful examples: Bitcoin and Ethereum (see Sect. 4.2.2). Centralized so-called private or private permissioned "blockchain" solutions or the distributed ledger solutions (e.g., IOTA) that emerged during the blockchain hype, relinquish decentralization for a scalable, highly efficient and secure solution. There has been movement away from the original ideas and goals of the Bitcoin and Ethereum blockchains and toward a return to the restrictions of user rights. These restrictions mean that users must authenticate and authorize themselves in order to use the system [32].

With respect to all of this, the question arises as to what can actually still be considered a blockchain. Just what can we call a blockchain and describe as blockchain-based? Does this term only refer to bitcoin-like projects that use the original parameters and goals or does it apply to a cryptographically referenced block chain?

In 2016 and 2017, when the blockchain hype had reached its peak, numerous companies took part in a "blockchain experiment." Each had its own, unique definition of blockchain, which meant that the hype surrounding blockchain technology had not only became a development driver, but also the most common cause of failure. The planning and development phase of many projects was drastically shortened to bring the product to the market in record time and to profit from the hype. Additionally, numerous technical concepts and projects that had already existed before blockchain technology (and had little to do with its innovation) were able to sell better under the name "blockchain." Consequently, it comes as no surprise that the widely-hyped blockchain technology has often been met with disappointment.

---

[5]The term was coined by Vitalik Buterin, the co-founder of Ethereum.

Even today[6] much discussion is going on about the "correct" definition of blockchain technology. In this book, we have focused on the innovation of blockchain technology and looked at the advantages this technology offers us when compared to existing, older solutions. Blockchain is neither a new encryption algorithm nor is it an "alien technology." Rather it is an innovative combination of existing technological approaches from cryptography, decentralized networks, and consensus-finding models. The focus remains on a robust and secure decentralized system, without restrictions placed on the number of system users or their identification.

A network designed on the basis of blockchain technology is often called an "Internet of Value." This term applies to the first generation of blockchain-based projects (bitcoin-like projects). In blockchain technology a value always has an owner. In the "blockchain register" the current state of the one who owns the value is documented. For this reason, blockchain technology is often compared to a public register.

With the second generation of blockchain-based projects comes the further development of the original concept of blockchain technology. Not only is a robust and secure decentralized system provided for the logging of value ownership, but the system acts as a large decentralized computer with millions of autonomous objects (smart contracts) that can maintain an internal database, execute code and communicate with each other [130]. Ethereum (it has existed since 2014), for example, is the first project of the second generation.

Both concepts are focused on updating and logging the respective state of the system. The first generation focuses on the current state of a value, meaning who owns a certain value (unspent transaction output – UTXO). Blockchain 2.0 targets the current state of an account (account state – balance, code, internal storage).

These accounts, for example in a Ethereum network, are divided into two types: external and internal accounts (see Sect. 4.1.1). Users of the Ethereum system have external accounts and, by means of transactions, can "transfer" Ether to other external accounts or activate internal accounts that are assigned to smart contracts. The smart contracts have an address and an account and their own code that controls them (for more on the subject of smart contracts see Sect. 5.1.2). The code can implement any rules or conditions and in this way map complex applications. These application run without any central "coordinator" at the computers of all full users (full nodes), and thus form a censor-resistant, decentralized world computer [38, 74, 130]. More complex smart contracts form so-called decentralized autonomous organizations (DAO), whose functions can be automatically executed depending on the predefined conditions.

Thus a blockchain-based system in its "original form" (public permissionless blockchain) makes sense when it comes to an application scenario in which numerous users who do not know or trust each other want to interact, and where there is no trust in a central authority or a middleman. For other scenarios, the

---

[6]At the time this book was written.

conventional solutions (such as a database) provide the more appropriate technology [32].

Supposing you have decided on a blockchain-based solution. The next step involves collecting further criteria, for example the cost-benefit ratio. This is the basis for deciding whether to implement an existing solution or to develop a solution of one's own (see Chap. 5). The next question applies to the actual goal or, more specifically, to the "content" of the application, namely: which interactions should take place between users? Is the focus of your application to securely capture and log the state (or more precisely the ownership) of a value? This could apply for instance to the ownership of securities, an object of art, a product or the logging of copyrights. In such cases a simple UTXO-based Blockchain 1.0 is sufficient. However, if you want your application to be more complex, an account-based Blockchain 2.0 is the better choice. For example, if the state of a value or an individual user account need to offer greater flexibility, or if your user interactions are tied to complex conditions that must be automatically controlled and executed. With the help of smart contracts, any number of complex applications – so-called decentralized applications or dApps for short – can be created and used decentrally without additional middlemen.

Whether a UTXO- or an account-based model should be used does not depend on the application area of blockchain technology but on the specific problem. Thereby, the focus and properties of the respective model need to be considered and the question raised as to whether they correspond to the concept at hand. It is advisable to first address the problem and only then to look for a suitable technology, which must be consequently fully explored to take advantage of its potential.

The development of a new blockchain offers great flexibility and freedom in the composition of the desired functionalities and rules. At the same time, this comes at the cost of development time and security, as any changes to the existing solutions could lead to security gaps and weaknesses. Since the source code of many blockchain-based systems is public, users are free to use it for their own blockchain applications and to adapt it according to their needs. Bitcoin, Ethereum and Hyperledger systems have become standards on the blockchain scene to a great extent.

Numerous projects and providers on the market support companies in their introduction of blockchain. In recent years, various consortia have emerged and developed solutions that offer "Blockchain-as-a-Service."[7] Blockchain technology has already taken over many application sectors, and increasingly more companies are offering ready-made solutions adapted to specific areas. At this time there is hardly any application area with a decentralized infrastructure in which an attempt has not been made to introduce blockchain.

The following are the most common application areas (see Chap. 6):

- Tracking a possession of a value,
- Joint control over specific values (Multi-Signature),

---

[7] A private blockchain is often used for this purpose.

- Voting,
- Automated contracts,
- Games, including gambling,
- Identity and reputation systems,
- Decentralized markets,
- Decentralized data storage or data processing,
- Decentralized autonomous organizations.

Thanks to broad practical use and intensive research, blockchain technology has undergone rapid development from the original use area of cryptocurrency (or a decentralized register) to that of a programmable decentralized trust infrastructure. During this time, blockchain technology has also provided impetus for further P2P solutions and served to promote the development of a user-controlled and long-lived twentyfirst century identity – and perhaps even advanced the missing identity layer of the Internet [43, 176].

With this book, we hope we have succeeded in helping you to answer your own questions about blockchain technology and its use, and that we have assisted you in reaching your own conclusions. We will have achieved our goal if you found the necessary information here to determine, what is truly innovative about blockchain technology, within the realm of your own experience, and what is little more than hype.

Appendix A
Byzantine Agreement Algorithm

The Byzantine Agreement Algorithm offers a solution to the Byzantine Generals Problem, and thus allows agreement between the nodes ("generals") in a synchronous system, a third of whose nodes are faulty or malicious. According to Lamport, [19] each node (computer, user) creates a vector with those values it has received from other nodes. After the vectors have been constructed, they are exchanged. Each node checks all the values obtained from each vector, makes a majority decision, and uses this as the result of the algorithm. In his work, Lamport uses two restrictions for the solution: the sending of verbal and signed messages. Because of this, two algorithms were developed (see [35]). Further restrictions must be made to use the algorithm in a distributed network of nodes with equal rights, whose number grows dynamically.

© Springer Nature Switzerland AG 2021
T. Gayvoronskaya, C. Meinel, *Blockchain*,
https://doi.org/10.1007/978-3-030-61559-8

Appendix B
Automatically Use TOR Hidden Services

Starting with Tor version 0.2.7.1 it is possible, through Tor's control socket API, to create and destroy "ephemeral" hidden services programmatically. Bitcoin Core has been updated to make use of this. This means that if Tor is running (and proper authorization is available), Bitcoin Core automatically creates a hidden service to listen on, without manual configuration. Bitcoin Core will also use Tor automatically to connect to other .onion nodes if the control socket can be successfully opened. This will positively affect the number of available .onion nodes and their usage.

This new feature is enabled by default if Bitcoin Core is listening, and a connection to Tor can be made. It can be configured with the -listenonion, -torcontrol and -torpassword settings. To show verbose debugging information, pass -debug= tor [54].

© Springer Nature Switzerland AG 2021
T. Gayvoronskaya, C. Meinel, *Blockchain*,
https://doi.org/10.1007/978-3-030-61559-8

Appendix C
Verifying the Transaction in the Bitcoin System

1. Check syntactic correctness.
2. Make sure neither in or out lists are empty.
3. Size in bytes < MAX_BLOCK_SIZE.
4. Each output value, as well as the total, must be in legal money range.
5. Make sure none of the inputs have hash $= 0$, $n = -1$ (coinbase transactions).
6. Check that nLockTime $<= INT\_MAX$, size in bytes $>= 100$, and sig opcount $<= 2$.
7. Reject "nonstandard" transactions: scriptSig doing anything other than pushing numbers on the stack, or scriptPubkey not matching the two usual forms.
8. Reject if we already have matching tx in the pool, or in a block in the main branch.
9. For each input, if the referenced output exists in any other tx in the pool, reject this transaction.
10. For each input, look in the main branch and the transaction pool to find the referenced output transaction. If the output transaction is missing for any input, this will be an orphan transaction. Add to the orphan transactions, if a matching transaction is not in there already.
11. For each input, if the referenced output transaction is coinbase (i.e. only 1 input, with hash $= 0$, $n = -1$), it must have at least COINBASE_MATURITY (100) confirmations; else reject this transaction.
12. For each input, if the referenced output does not exist (e.g. never existed or has already been spent), reject this transaction.
13. Using the referenced output transactions to get input values, check that each input value, as well as the sum, are in legal money range.
14. Reject if the sum of input values < sum of output values.
15. Reject if transaction fee (defined as sum of input values minus sum of output values) would be too low to get into an empty block.
16. Verify the scriptPubKey accepts for each input; reject if any are bad.
17. Add to transaction pool.

© Springer Nature Switzerland AG 2021
T. Gayvoronskaya, C. Meinel, *Blockchain*,
https://doi.org/10.1007/978-3-030-61559-8

18. Add to wallet if mine.
19. Relay transaction to peers.
20. For each orphan transaction that uses this one as one of its inputs, run all these steps (including this one) recursively on that orphan [64].

Appendix D
The Byzantine Generals Problem

We imagine that several divisions of the Byzantine army are camped outside an enemy city, each division commanded by its own general. The generals can communicate with one another only by messenger. After observing the enemy, they must decide upon a common plan of action. However, some of the generals may be traitors, trying to prevent the loyal generals from reaching agreement. The generals must have an algorithm to guarantee that

1. all loyal generals decide upon the same plan of action. The loyal generals will all do what the algorithm says they should, but the traitors may do anything they wish. The algorithm must guarantee condition A regardless of what the traitors do. The loyal generals should not only reach agreement, but should agree upon a reasonable plan. We therefore also want to insure that
2. a small number of traitors cannot cause the loyal generals to adopt a bad plan [19].

© Springer Nature Switzerland AG 2021
T. Gayvoronskaya, C. Meinel, *Blockchain*,
https://doi.org/10.1007/978-3-030-61559-8

Appendix E
Atomic Cross-Chain Trading

A and B are two Nodes, that hold Units (coins) on different blockchains.

A picks a random number x

A creates TX1: "Pay w BTC to <B's public key> if (x for H(x) known and signed by B) or (signed by A & B)"

A creates TX2: "Pay w BTC from TX1 to <A's public key>, locked 48 hours in the future"

A sends TX2 to B

B signs TX2 and returns to A

1. A submits TX1 to the network

    B creates TX3: "Pay v alt-coins to <A-public-key> if (x for H(x) known and signed by A) or (signed by A & B)"

    B creates TX4: "Pay v alt-coins from TX3 to <B's public key>, locked 24 hours in the future"

    B sends TX4 to A

    A signs TX4 and sends back to B
2. B submits TX3 to the network
3. A spends TX3 giving x
4. B spends TX1 using x

This is atomic (with timeout). If the process is halted, it can be reversed no matter when it is stopped.

Before 1: Nothing public has been broadcast, so nothing happens

Between 1 & 2: A can use refund transaction after 48 hours to get his money back

Between 2 & 3: B can get refund after 24 hours. A has 24 more hours to get his refund

After 3: Transaction is completed by 2

- A must spend his new coin within 24 hours or B can claim the refund and keep his coins

© Springer Nature Switzerland AG 2021
T. Gayvoronskaya, C. Meinel, *Blockchain*,
https://doi.org/10.1007/978-3-030-61559-8

- B must spend his new coin within 48 hours or A can claim the refund and keep his coins

For safety, both should complete the process with lots of time until the deadlines [71].

Appendix F
Ethereum Roadmap

Ethereum 2.0 (Serenity) Phases [116, 131]

Design Goals

- Decentralization: to allow for a typical consumer laptop with $O(C)$ resources to process/validate $O(1)$ shards (including any system level validation such as the beacon chain).
- Resilience: to remain live through major network partitions and when very large portions of nodes go offline.
- Security: to utilize crypto and design techniques that allow for a large participation of validators in total and per unit time.
- Simplicity: to minimize complexity, even at the cost of some losses in efficiency.
- Longevity: to select all components such that they are either quantum secure or can be easily swapped out for quantum secure counterparts when available.

Phase 0

- The Beacon Chain.
- Fork Choice.
- Deposit Contract.
- Honest Validator.

Phase 1

- Custody Game.
- Shard Data Chains.
- Misc beacon chain updates.

Phase 2

- Phase 2 is still actively in Research and Development and does not yet have any formal specifications.
- See the Eth 2.0 Phase 2 Wiki for current progress, discussions, and definitions.

© Springer Nature Switzerland AG 2021
T. Gayvoronskaya, C. Meinel, *Blockchain*,
https://doi.org/10.1007/978-3-030-61559-8

References

1. Adapted according to M. Ali, J. Nelson, R. Shea, M.J. Freedman, Blockstack: A global naming and storage system secured by blockchains, in *2016 USENIX Annual Technical Conference, USENIX ATC 16, 2016*, pp. 181–194; with the kind permission of Blockstack PBC. All Rights Reserved
2. M. Bastiaan, *Preventing the 51%-attack: a stochastic analysis of two phase proof of work in bitcoin* (2015)
3. F.L. Bauer, *Entzifferte Geheimnisse: Methoden und Maximen der Kryptologie* (Springer, Berlin/Heidelberg, 2000), p. 27
4. A. Biryukov, D. Khovratovich, I. Pustogarov, Deanonymisation of clients in Bitcoin P2P network, in *Proceedings of the 2014 ACM SIGSAC Conference on Computer and Communications Security* (ACM, 2014), pp. 15–29
5. BitFury Group, *Proof of Stake versus Proof of Work*, (White Paper, Sep 13, 2015 (Version 1.0)), pp. 1–26
6. G. Caronni, Walking the web of trust, in *Proceedings IEEE 9th International Workshops on Enabling Technologies: Infrastructure for Collaborative Enterprises (WET ICE 2000)*, pp. 153–158
7. M. Castro, B. Liskov, Practical Byzantine fault tolerance, in *Proceedings of the Third Symposium on Operating Systems Design and Implementation*, New Orleans, Feb 1999, vol. 99, pp. 173–186
8. S. De Angelis, L. Aniello, R. Baldoni, F. Lombardi, A. Margheri, V. Sassone *PBFT vs Proof-of-Authority: Applying the CAP Theorem to Permissioned Blockchain* (2018)
9. Z. Despotovic, K. Aberer, *Possibilities for Managing Trust in P2P Networks* (Swiss Federal Institute of Technology – EPFL, 2004)
10. B. Eylert, *Zugangssicherung* (Sicherheit in der Informationstechnik, News & Media, Berlin, 2012), pp. 12–19
11. B. Eylert, D. Eylert, *Ausgewählte Verschlüsselungsverfahren* (Sicherheit in der Informationstechnik, News & Media, Berlin, 2012), pp. 67–83
12. B. Eylert, J. Mohnke, *Signaturverfahren* (Sicherheit in der Informationstechnik, News & Media, Berlin, 2012), pp. 84–90
13. P. Franco, *Understanding Bitcoin: Cryptography, Engineering and Economics* (Wiley, New York, 2014)
14. R. Guha, R. Kumar, P. Raghavan, A. Tomkins, Propagation of trust and distrust, in *Proceedings of the 13th International Conference on World Wide Web* (ACM, 2004), pp. 403–412
15. P. Jogalekar, M. Woodside, Evaluating the scalability of distributed systems, in *IEEE Transactions on Parallel and Distributed Systems* (IEEE, 2000), vol. 11, pp. 589–603

© Springer Nature Switzerland AG 2021
T. Gayvoronskaya, C. Meinel, *Blockchain*,
https://doi.org/10.1007/978-3-030-61559-8

16. A. Kerckhoffs, La cryptographie militaire. Journal des sciences militaires **9**, 161–191 (1883)
17. S. Kim, Y. Kwon, S. Cho, A survey of scalability solutions on blockchain, in *International Conference on Information and Communication Technology Convergence (ICTC)* (IEEE, 2018), pp. 1204–1207
18. S. King, S. Nadal, *Ppcoin: Peer-to-peer crypto-currency with Proof-of-Stake* (self-published paper, 2012)
19. L. Lamport, R. Shostak, M. Pease, The Byzantine generals problem. ACM Trans. Program. Lang. Syst. **4.3**, 382–401 (1982)
20. S.D. Lerner, *Rootstock – Bitcoin powered Smart Contracts* (the-blockchain.com, 2015)
21. X. Li, P. Jiang, T. Chen, X. Luo, Q. Wen, *A Survey on the Security of Blockchain Systems* (Future Generation Computer Systems, Elsevier, 2017)
22. L. Luu, D. Chu, H. Olickel, P. Saxena, A. Hobor, Making smart contracts smarter, in *Proceedings of the 2016 ACM SIGSAC Conference on Computer and Communications Security, 2016*, pp. 254–269
23. D. Mazières, *The Stellar Consensus Protocol: A Federated Model for Internet-level Consensus* (2016)
24. C. Meinel, T. Gayvoronskaya, A. Mühle, *Die Zukunftspotenziale der Blockchain-Technologie*, published by E. Böttinger, J. Zu Putlitz. Die Zukunft der Medizin, vol. 1 (Medizinisch Wissenschaftliche Verlagsgesellschaft, Berlin, 2019), pp. 259–268
25. C. Meinel, T. Gayvoronskaya, M. Schnjakin, *Blockchain: Hype or Innovation*, vol. 124 (Universitätsverlag Potsdam, Potsdam, 2018)
26. S. Nakamoto, *Bitcoin: A peer-to-peer electronic cash system* (2008)
27. G. Pappalardo, T. Di Matteo, G. Caldarelli, T. Aste, Blockchain inefficiency in the Bitcoin peers network. EPJ Data Sci. **7**, 1–13 (2018)
28. R. Pass, L. Seeman, A. Shelat, Analysis of the blockchain protocol in asynchronous networks, in *Annual International Conference on the Theory and Applications of Cryptographic Techniques* (Springer, Cham, 2017), pp. 643–673
29. P. Pesch, R. Böhme, *Datenschutz trotz öffentlicher Blockchain*, vol. 41 (Datenschutz und Datensicherheit-DuD, Springer, 2017), pp. 93–98
30. J. Poon, T. Dryja, *The bitcoin lightning network: Scalable off-chain instant payments*, (Technical Report (draft). https://lightning.network, 2015)
31. M. Rosenfeld, *Analysis of hashrate-based double spending* (arXiv preprint arXiv:1402.2009, 2014)
32. M. Scherer, *Performance and Scalability of Blockchain Networks and Smart Contracts* (Umea University, Umea, 2017)
33. Y. Sompolinsky, A. Zohar, Secure high-rate transaction processing in bitcoin, in *International Conference on Financial Cryptography and Data Security* (Springer, 2015), pp. 507–527
34. N. Szabo, Formalizing and securing relationships on public networks. First Monday **2**(9) (1997), https://doi.org/10.5210/fm.v2i9.548
35. D.M. Toth, *The Byzantine Agreement Protocol Applied to Security* (Worcester Polytechnic Institute, 2004)
36. M. Walker et al., *Gartner Inc. – Gartner "Hype Cycle for Emerging Technologies, 2016"* (19 July 2016)
37. M. Walker, *Gartner Inc. – Gartner "Hype Cycle for Emerging Technologies, 2017"* (21 July 2017)
38. G. Wood, *Ethereum: a secure decentralised generalised transaction ledger* (EIP-150 Revision, 2014)
39. *3sat – Bitcoin, der Wert der digitalen Währung schwankt extrem*, http://www.3sat.de/page/? source=/nano/glossar/bitcoin.html. Visited on 14 Sept 2017
40. *Academic – Produkt (Wirtschaft)*, https://deacademic.com/dic.nsf/dewiki/1133058# Angebotsorientierte_Definition. Visited on 01 May 2019
41. *Adobe Blog – Wie Estland zum Digital Government-Vorreiter in Europa wurde*, https://blogs. adobe.com/digitaleurope/de/governmental-affairs/wie-estland-zum-digital-government-vorreiter-in-europa-wurde/. Visited on 01 Dec 2019

42. *Agrello – Solutions*, https://www.agrello.io/#solutions. Visited on 01 Dec 2019
43. C. Allen, in *The Path to Self-Sovereign Identity*, https://github.com/WebOfTrustInfo/self-sovereign-identity/blob/master/ThePathToSelf-SovereignIdentity.md. Visited on 1 Dec 2019
44. B. Asolo, in *ScriptPubKey & ScriptSig Explained*, Mycryptopedia, https://www.mycryptopedia.com/scriptpubkey-scriptsig/. Visited on 20 Nov 2018
45. N. Azimdoust, in *Blockchainwelt – ERC-20 Token Standard einfach erklärt, April 2019*, https://blockchainwelt.de/erc20-token-ethereum-einfach-erklaert/. Visited on 04 Sept 2019
46. A. Back, M. Corallo, L. Dashjr, M. Friedenbach, G. Maxwell, A. Miller, A. Poelstra, J. Timón, P. Wuille in *Enabling blockchain innovations with pegged sidechains*. http://www.opensciencereview.com/papers/123/enablingblockchain-innovations-with-pegged-sidechains (2014)
47. *BCCC – Member company*, https://bccc.global/wp/about/company/. Visited on 26 Nov 2019
48. *Bdrive – Simple and secure data storage and sharing in the cloud*, https://www.bundesdruckerei.de/en/solutions/Bdrive. Visited on 01 Dec 2019
49. *Bdrive Sicherheit – Whitepaper*, https://www.bundesdruckerei.de/de/WP-Detailseite-Bdrive-Sicherheit-0. Visited on 01 Dec 2019
50. *Bitcoin – Bitcoin Developer Reference*, https://bitcoin.org/en/developer-reference#block-chain. Visited on 17 Apr 2017
51. *Bitcoin – Contracts*, https://bitcoin.org/en/contracts-guide#micropayment-channel. Visited on am 22 Aug 2019
52. *Bitcoin – Protect your privacy*, https://bitcoin.org/en/protect-your-privacy. Visited on 17 Apr 2017
53. *Bitcoin – Securing your wallet*, https://bitcoin.org/en/secure-your-wallet. Visited on 01 Dec 2019
54. *Bitcoin – Automatically use TOR Hidden Services*, https://bitcoin.org/en/release/v0.12.0. Visited on 01 Dec 2019
55. *Bitcoin Wiki – Address*, https://en.bitcoin.it/wiki/Address. Visited on 18 Apr 2017
56. *Bitcoin Wiki – BIP*, https://en.bitcoin.it/wiki/Bitcoin_Improvement_Proposals. Visited on 18 Apr 2017
57. *Bitcoin Wiki – Bitcoin Core*, https://en.bitcoin.it/wiki/Bitcoin_Core. Visited on 18 Apr 2017
58. *Bitcoin Wiki – Common Vulnerabilities and Exposures*, https://en.bitcoin.it/wiki/Common_Vulnerabilities_and_Exposures. Visited on 10 June 2019
59. *Bitcoin Wiki – Transaction*, https://en.bitcoin.it/wiki/Transaction. Visited on 01 Dec 2019
60. *Bitcoin Wiki – Hardware wallet*, https://en.bitcoin.it/wiki/Hardware_wallet. Visited on 01 Dec 2019
61. *Bitcoin Wiki – Main page*, https://en.bitcoin.it/wiki/Main_Page. Visited on 01 Dec 2019
62. *Bitcoin Wiki – Mining*, https://en.bitcoin.it/wiki/Mining. Visited on 01 Dec 2019
63. *Bitcoin Wiki – Multisignature*, https://en.bitcoin.it/wiki/Multisignature. Visited on 18 Apr 2017
64. *Bitcoin Wiki – Protocol rules*, https://en.bitcoin.it/wiki/Protocol_rules. Visited on 01 Dec 2019
65. *Bitcoin Wiki – Setting up a Tor hidden service*, https://en.bitcoin.it/wiki/Setting_up_a_Tor_hidden_service. Visited on 20 May 2019
66. *Bitcoin Wiki – Script*, https://en.bitcoinwiki.org/wiki/Script. Visited on 20 Nov 2018
67. *Bitcoin Wiki – Weaknesses*, https://en.bitcoin.it/wiki/Weaknesses. Visited on 10 June 2019
68. *Bitcoin-Blase – Was sind Stablecoins*, https://www.bitcoinblase.at/was-sind-stablecoins/. Visited on 20 Nov 2019
69. *BitcoinBlog.de – Adressen bei Kryptowährungen: eine Einführung*, https://bitcoinblog.de/2017/06/12/adressen-bei-kryptowaehrungen-eine-einfuehrung. Visited on 17 Apr 2017
70. *BitcoinBlog.de – Ein Startup, Sybils Angriff und die Privatsphäre*, https://bitcoinblog.de/2015/03/19/ein-startup-sybils-angriff-und-die-privatsphare/. Visited on 01 Dec 2019
71. *Bitcointalk.org*, https://bitcointalk.org/index.php?topic=193281.msg2224949#msg2224949. Visited on 01 Dec 2019

72. *Bitinfocharts – Bitcoin Transactions historical chart*, https://bitinfocharts.com/comparison/bitcoin-transactions.html. Visited on 01 Dec 2019

73. *Bitinfocharts – Ethereum Transactions historical chart*, https://bitinfocharts.com/comparison/ethereum-transactions.html. Visited on 01 Dec 2019

74. *Bits on Blocks – A gentle introduction to Ethereum*, https://bitsonblocks.net/2016/10/02/gentle-introduction-ethereum/. Visited on 12 Feb 2019

75. *Blockchain Bundesverband – New Position Paper: Self Sovereign Identity defined*, https://bundesblock.de/de/new-position-paper-self-sovereign-identity-defined/. Visited on 1 Dec 2019

76. *Blockchain Bundesverband – Self-sovereign Identity: a position paper on blockchain enabled identity and the road ahead*, https://www.bundesblock.de/wp-content/uploads/2019/01/ssi-paper.pdf. Visited on 1 Dec 2019

77. *Blockchain.com – Confirmed Transactions Per Day*, https://www.blockchain.com/charts/n-transactions. Visited on 01 Aug 2019

78. *Blockchain.com – Total Hash Rate (TH/s)*, https://www.blockchain.com/charts/hash-rate. Visited on 01 Dec 2019

79. *Blockchain.com – Hashrate distribution amongst the largest mining pools*, https://www.blockchain.com/charts/pools. Visited on 01 Dec 2019

80. *Blockgeeks – Blockchain Glossary: From A–Z*, https://blockgeeks.com/guides/blockchain-glossary-from-a-z/. Visited on 01 Dec 2019

81. *Blockgeeks – Smart Contracts: The Blockchain Technology That Will Replace Lawyers*, https://blockgeeks.com/guides/smart-contracts/. Visited on 01 Dec 2019

82. *Blockstack – Blockstack Technical Whitepaper v 2.0*, https://blockstack.org/whitepaper.pdf. Visited on 1 Dec 2019

83. *Blockstack – Easily build blockchain apps that scale*, https://blockstack.org/technology. Visited on 1 Dec 2019

84. *Brooklyn Microgrid – Overview*, https://www.brooklyn.energy/about. Visited on 1 Dec 2019

85. *BTC-Echo – Schweden nutzt jetzt offiziell die Blockchain für Grundbucheintragungen*, https://www.btc-echo.de/schweden-nutzt-jetzt-offiziell-die-blockchain-fuer-grundbucheintragungen/. Visited on 25 Nov 2019

86. *BTC-Echo – So viel Geld benötigst du für eine Bitcoin 51 Prozent Attacke*, https://www.btc-echo.de/so-viel-geld-benoetigst-du-fuer-eine-bitcoin-51-attacke/. Visited on 01 Dec 2019

87. *Bundesblock – Blockchain Bundesverband*, http://bundesblock.de/2017/10/17/bundesverband-veroeffentlicht-positionspapier/. Visited on 01 Dec 2019

88. *Bundesdruckerei GmbH – How digital identities work*, https://www.bundesdruckerei.de/en/Themen-Trends/Magazin/Was-ist-eine-digitale-Identitaet. Visited on 1 Dec 2019

89. *Federal Ministry for Economic Affairs and Energy – Blockchain Strategy of the Federal Government*, https://www.bmwi.de/Redaktion/EN/Publikationen/Digitale-Welt/blockchain-strategy.html. Visited on 20 Nov 2019

90. *Bundesministerium der Wirtschaft und Energie und Bundesministerium der Finanzen – Online-Konsultation zur Erarbeitung der Blockchain-Strategie der Bundesregierung*, https://www.bmwi.de/Redaktion/DE/Downloads/B/blockchain-strategie.pdf?__blob=publicationFile&v=4. Visited on 20 Nov 2019

91. *CBInsights Research Portal – Blockchain Trends In Review*, https://www.cbinsights.com/research/report/blockchain-trends-opportunities/. Visited on 27 Nov 2019

92. *ClearKarma*, http://www.clearkarma.com/. Visited on 01 Dec 2019

93. *Clearmatics – Building the decentralised Financial Market Infrastructure (dFMI) of the Future*, https://www.clearmatics.com/about/. Visited on 26 Nov 2019

94. *CoinDesk – Coalition Launches to Promote Blockchain in the Netherlands*, https://www.coindesk.com/coalition-launches-promote-blockchain-netherlands. Visited on 25 Nov 2019

95. *CoinDesk – How Bitcoin's Technology Could Reshape Our Medical Experiences*, http://www.coindesk.com/bitcoin-technology-could-reshape-medical-experiences/. Visited on 01 Dec 2019

96. *Colony – Technical White Paper*, https://colony.io/whitepaper.pdf. Visited on 01 Nov 2019

97. *Consensys – Blockchain and The Energy Industry*, https://media.consensys.net/the-state-of-energy-blockchain-37268e053bbd. Visited on 1 Dec 2019
98. V. Costea, in *Bitcoin Magazine – Video Interview: Giacomo Zucco and RGB Tokens Built on Bitcoin, Aug 2019*, https://bitcoinmagazine.com/articles/video-interview-giacomo-zucco-rgb-tokens-built-bitcoin. Visited on 03 Sept 2019
99. *Coinmap.org*, https://coinmap.org/view/. Visited on 13 May 2020
100. *CryptoCompare – What is merged mining – Bitcoin & Namecoin – Litecoin & Dogecoin*, https://www.cryptocompare.com/mining/guides/what-is-merged-mining-bitcoin-namecoin-litecoin-dogecoin/. Visited on 01 Dec 2019
101. *Datarella – Eine Dezentrale Autonome Organisation DAO – Was ist das*, http://datarella.de/dezentrale-autonome-organisation-dao-was-ist-das/. Visited on 20 Oct 2017
102. *Deloitte – Blockchain from a perspective of data protection law*, https://www2.deloitte.com/dl/en/pages/legal/articles/blockchain-datenschutzrecht.html. Visited on 20 May 2019
103. *DerTreasurer – Daimler platziert Schuldschein via Blockchain*, https://www.dertreasurer.de/news/finanzen-bilanzen/daimler-platziert-schuldschein-via-blockchain-58651/. Visited on 26 Nov 2019
104. *Duden*, https://www.duden.de/. Visited on 15 Apr 2019
105. *Dutch Blockchain Coalition – About the Dutch Blockchain Coalition*, https://dutchblockchaincoalition.org/en/about-dbc. Visited on 25 Nov 2019
106. *E-Estonia*, https://e-estonia.com/. Visited on 01 Dec 2017
107. *E-Estonia – KSI Blockchain*, https://e-estonia.com/solutions/security-and-safety/ksi-blockchain/. Visited on 25 Nov 2019
108. B. Edgington, in *State of Ethereum Protocol #2: The Beacon Chain*, Medium – ConsenSys, https://docs.ethhub.io/ethereum-roadmap/ethereum-2.0/sharding/. Visited on 20 Aug 2019
109. *ElectricChain – Home*, https://www.electricchain.org/. Visited on 1 Dec 2019
110. *Eterna Capital – Blockchain Based Decentralised Cloud Computing*, https://medium.com/@eternacapital/blockchain-based-decentralised-cloud-computing-277f307611e1. Visited on 26 Nov 2019
111. *Ethereum Yellow Paper*, https://github.com/ethereum/yellowpaper. Visited on 01 Dec 2019
112. *Etherscan.io – Ethereum Average Block Size Chart*, https://etherscan.io/chart/blocksize. Visited on 01 Dec 2019
113. *Etherscan.io – Ethereum Block Time History*, https://etherscan.io/chart/blocktime. Visited on 15 Aug 2019
114. *Etherscan.io – Ethereum Daily Transactions Chart*, https://etherscan.io/chart/tx. Visited on 01 Dec 2019
115. *Etherscan.org – Total number of transactions per day*, https://www.etherchain.org/charts/transactionsPerDay. Visited on 01 Dec 2019
116. *EthHub – Ethereum Roadmap – Ethereum 2.0 (Serenity) Phases*, https://docs.ethhub.io/ethereum-roadmap/ethereum-2.0/eth-2.0-phases/. Visited on 20 Aug 2019
117. *EthHub – Ethereum Roadmap – Sharding*, https://docs.ethhub.io/ethereum-roadmap/ethereum-2.0/sharding/. Visited on 20 Aug 2019
118. *EthHub – Ethereum Roadmap – State Channels*, https://docs.ethhub.io/ethereum-roadmap/layer-2-scaling/state-channels/. Visited on 20 Aug 2019
119. *EthHub – Ethereum Roadmap – Plasma*, https://docs.ethhub.io/ethereum-roadmap/layer-2-scaling/plasma/. Visited on 20 Aug 2019
120. *EthHub – Using Ethereum – Running an Ethereum Node*, https://docs.ethhub.io/using-ethereum/running-an-ethereum-node/#full-nodes. Visited on 17 Aug 2019
121. *EthHub – Using Ethereum – Running an Ethereum Node*, https://docs.ethhub.io/using-ethereum/running-an-ethereum-node/#client-settings_2. Visited on 1 Dec 2019
122. *EU Blockchain Observatory and Forum – Map*, https://www.eublockchainforum.eu/initiative-map. Visited on 25 Nov 2019
123. *Gartner Inc. – Gartner-Methodologies – general graphic of Gartner Hype Cycle 2020*, https://www.gartner.com/en/research/methodologies/gartner-hype-cycle (With friendly permission of Gartner, Inc. and/or its affiliates. All rights reserved)

124. *Gem – Health*, https://gem.co/health/ (With friendly permission of Gem®)
125. *GitHub – Bitcoin/bips – BIP 141*, https://github.com/bitcoin/bips/blob/master/bip-0141. mediawiki. Visited on 15 Aug 2019
126. *Github – Colored Coins Protocol Specification*, https://github.com/Colored-Coins/Colored-Coins-Protocol-Specification/wiki/Introduction. Visited on 01 Dec 2019
127. *GitHub – Ethereum – A Next-Generation Smart Contract and Decentralized Application Platform*, https://github.com/ethereum/wiki/wiki/White-Paper. Visited on 03 May 2019
128. *GitHub – Ethereum – Design Rationale*, https://github.com/ethereum/wiki/wiki/Design-Rationale#gas-and-fees. Visited on 15 Aug 2019
129. *GitHub – Ethereum – EIPs – EIP-20*, https://github.com/ethereum/EIPs/blob/master/EIPS/eip-20.md. Visited on 03 Sept 2019
130. *GitHub – Ethereum – Ethereum Development Tutorial*, https://github.com/ethereum/wiki/wiki/Ethereum-Development-Tutorial. Visited on 03 May 2019
131. *GitHub – Ethereum – Ethereum 2.0 Specifications*, https://github.com/ethereum/eth2.0-specs. Visited on 20 Aug 2019
132. *GitHub – Ethereum – Mining*, https://github.com/ethereum/wiki/wiki/Mining. Visited on 03 May 2019
133. *GitHub – Ethereum – Patricia Tree*, https://github.com/ethereum/wiki/wiki/Patricia-Tree. Visited on 03 May 2019
134. *GitHub – Ethereum – Sharding introduction R&D compendium*, https://github.com/ethereum/wiki/wiki/Sharding-introduction-R&D-compendium. Visited on 15 Aug 2019
135. *Guardtime – Our Technology*, https://guardtime.com/technology. Visited on 14 Oct 2017
136. *Guardtime-Federal – Keyless Signature Infrastructure*, https://www.guardtime-federal.com/ksi/. Visited on 25 Nov 2019
137. *Handelsblatt – Strom aus der Nachbarschaft*, http://www.handelsblatt.com/technik/energie-umwelt/circular-economy/transactive-grid-mikronetzwerk-fuer-zehn-haeuserblocks/14793648-2.html. Visited on 01 Dec 2019
138. *Heise Security – Sicherheit der Verschlüsselung*, https://m.heise.de/security/artikel/Kryptographie-in-der-IT-Empfehlungen-zu-Verschluesselung-und-Verfahren-3221002.html?artikelseite=all. Visited on 01 Dec 2019
139. *Hsiao-Wei Wang – Presentation "Ethereum, Serenity"*, With friendly permission of Hsiao-Wei Wang
140. *Hyperledger – Frameworks*, https://www.hyperledger.org/. Visited on 01 Dec 2019
141. *IBM – Watson Internet of Things*, http://www.ibm.com/internet-of-things/iot-news/announcements/private-blockchain/. Visited on 04 Jan 2017
142. *IBM News Room – Maersk and IBM Introduce TradeLens Blockchain Shipping Solution*, https://newsroom.ibm.com/2018-08-09-Maersk-and-IBM-Introduce-TradeLens-Blockchain-Shipping-Solution. Visited on 1 Dec 2019
143. *International Business Times – Filament evolving entire IoT space using Bitcoin blockchain*, http://www.ibtimes.co.uk/filament-evolving-entire-iot-space-underwhelming-use-blockchain-1579096. Visited on 01 Dec 2019
144. *ITWissen.info – Peer-to-Peer-Netz*, http://www.itwissen.info/Peer-to-Peer-Netz-peer-to-peer-network-P2P.html. Visited on 01 Dec 2019
145. *Jolocom – Own your digital self*, https://jolocom.io/. Visited on 1 Dec 2019
146. *JuraForum – Analogieverbot - Erklärung, Beispiele und wann das Analogieverbot gilt*, https://www.juraforum.de/lexikon/analogieverbot. Visited on 20 May 2019
147. *O. Kuhlemann, in Kryptografie*, Kryptografie.de, http://kryptografie.de/kryptografie/index.htm. Visited on 06 Mar 2019
148. *Landau Microgrid Project*, https://im.iism.kit.edu/1093_2058.php. Visited on 01 Dec 2019
149. *LEADVISE Reply – DAO – Dezentrale Autonome Organisationen*, http://www.leadvise.de/latest-thinking/blockchain/dao-dezentrale-autonome-organisationen/. Visited on 01 Dec 2019
150. *Learn me a bitcoin – Difficulty*, http://learnmeabitcoin.com/guide/difficulty. Visited on 01 Dec 2019

151. *Ledger SAS – Image of Ledger Nano X*, (With friendly permission of © Ledger SAS. All rights reserved)
152. *Let's Talk Payments – Know more about Blockchain: Overview, Technology, Application Areas and Use Cases*, https://letstalkpayments.com/an-overview-of-blockchain-technology/. Visited on 01 Dec 2019
153. K. Li in *Hackernoon – Ethereum's ERC-20 Tokens Explained, Simply, October 2019*, https://hackernoon.com/ethereums-erc-20-tokens-explained-simply-88f5f8a7ae90. Visited on 20 Oct 2019
154. *Lightning Network Community Blog – Alpha Release of the Lightning Network Daemon*, https://lightning.community/release/software/lnd/lightning/2017/01/10/lightning-network-daemon-alpha-release/. Visited on am 22 Aug 2019
155. *Logistik Heute – Blockchain: Pilotprojekt zur Containerlogistik*, https://logistik-heute.de/news/blockchain-pilotprojekt-zur-containerlogistik-15175.html. Visited on 1 Dec 2019
156. *Mining Champ – Hashrate of Graphics Cards*, https://miningchamp.com/. Visited on 09 May 2019
157. *Modum.io*, https://modum.io/. Visited on 01 Dec 2019
158. *OpenBazaar – Buy and Sell Freely*, https://openbazaar.org/. Visited on 15 Oct 2019
159. *OpenBazaar – Escrow Smart Contract, Specification in OpenBazaar*, https://openbazaar.org/blog/Escrow-Smart-Contract-Specification-in-OpenBazaar/. Visited on 15 Oct 2019
160. *Oraclize.it – Ethereum Proof of Identity*, http://dapps.oraclize.it/proof-of-identity/. Visited on 14 Oct 2017
161. *Parity Technologies – Wiki – Proof-of-Authority Chains*, https://wiki.parity.io/Proof-of-Authority-Chains. Visited on 06 Oct 2019
162. *Port of Rotterdam – First blockchain container shipped to Rotterdam*, https://www.portofrotterdam.com/en/news-and-press-releases/first-blockchain-container-shipped-to-rotterdam. Visited on 1 Dec 2019
163. *Posttip.de – Lexikon – Produkt*, http://www.posttip.de/lexikon/produkt/. Visited on 01 May 2019
164. *Provable Things – Oraclize* (With friendly permission of Provable Things Limited. © All rights reserved)
165. *R3 – Who we are*, https://www.r3.com/about/. Visited on 26 Nov 2019
166. *Raiden Network – What is the Raiden Network*, https://raiden.network/101.html. Visited on 25 Aug 2019
167. *SCF Briefing – Foxconn uses blockchain for new SCF platform after 6,5 million dollar pilot*, http://www.scfbriefing.com/foxconn-launches-scf-blockchain-platform/. Visited on 01 Dec 2019
168. K. Schiller in *Ethereum 2.0 erscheint am 03.01.2020 – Was ist Serenity*, Blockchainwelt, https://blockchainwelt.de/ethereum-2-0-consensys-roadmap-serenity/. Visited on 20 Aug 2019
169. *SelfKey – Financial Services Signup made easy*, https://selfkey.org/. Visited on 1 Dec 2019
170. *Silicon – Neue Initiative will IoT mit Blockchain sicherer machen*, http://www.silicon.de/41639843/neue-initiative-will-iot-mit-blockchain-sicherer-machen/?inf_by=59799667671db810758b4634. Visited on 01 Dec 2019
171. *Slock.it – Concept*, https://in3.readthedocs.io/en/develop/intro.html. Visited on 1 Dec 2019
172. *Slock.it – In3*, https://github.com/slockit/in3. Visited on 1 Dec 2019
173. *Slock.it – Incubed Client*, https://slock.it/incubed/. Visited on 1 Dec 2019
174. *Slock.it – Use cases*, https://slock.it/use-cases/. Visited on 1 Dec 2019
175. *Sovrin – Control Your Digital Identity*, https://sovrin.org/. Visited on 1 Dec 2019
176. *Sovrin – The Inevitable Rise of Self-Sovereign Identity*, https://sovrin.org/wp-content/uploads/2018/03/The-Inevitable-Rise-of-Self-Sovereign-Identity.pdf. Visited on 1 Dec 2019

177. *SSI Meetup – Decentralized Identifiers (DIDs): The Fundamental Building Block of Self-Sovereign Identity (SSI)*, https://www.slideshare.net/SSIMeetup/decentralized-identifiers-dids-the-fundamental-building-block-of-selfsovereign-identity-ssi. Visited on 1 Dec 2019

178. *StackExchange – What is the difference between a smart contract and a DAO*, http://ethereum.stackexchange.com/questions/3336/what-is-the-difference-between-a-smart-contract-and-a-dao/4240. Visited on 01 Dec 2019

179. *Steem – An incentivized, blockchain-based, public content platform*, https://steem.com/steem-whitepaper.pdf. Visited on 15 Oct 2019

180. *Storj.io – Storj*, https://storj.io/. Visited on 26 Nov 2019

181. *Storj.io – Storj: A Decentralized Cloud Storage Network*, https://storj.io/storjv3.pdf. Visited on 26 Nov 2019

182. *TechCrunch – Decentralizing IoT networks through blockchain*, https://techcrunch.com/2016/06/28/decentralizing-iot-networks-through-blockchain/. Visited on 01 Dec 2019

183. *Tor Project – TOR*, https://www.torproject.org. Visited on 20 May 2019

184. *Tor Project – Tor: Hidden Service Protocol*, https://www.torproject.org/docs/hidden-services.html.en. Visited on 20 May 2019

185. *TradeLens – Solution Architecture*, https://docs.tradelens.com/learn/solution_architecture/. Visited on 1 Dec 2019

186. *SatoshiLabs – Image of Trezor One*, (With friendly permission of SatoshiLabs s.r.o. © All rights reserved)

187. *uPort – We build trust, so you can grow business, ecosystems, customers, communities*, https://www.uport.me/. Visited on 1 Dec 2019

188. A. Van Wirdum, in *Bitcoin Magazine – Segregated Witness, Part 1: How a Clever Hack Could Significantly Increase Bitcoin's Potential, Dec 2015*, https://bitcoinmagazine.com/articles/segregated-witness-part-how-a-clever-hack-could-significantly-increase-bitcoin-s-potential-1450553618. Visited on 15 Aug 2019

189. A. Van Wirdum, in *Bitcoin Magazine – Segregated Witness, Part 2: Why You Should Care About a Nitty-Gritty Technical Trick, Dec 2015*, https://bitcoinmagazine.com/articles/segregated-witness-part-why-you-should-care-about-a-nitty-gritty-technical-trick-1450827675. Visited on 15 Aug 2019

190. A. Van Wirdum, in *Bitcoin Magazine – Segregated Witness, Part 3: How a Soft Fork Might Establish a Block-Size Truce (or Not), Dec 2015*, https://bitcoinmagazine.com/articles/segregated-witness-part-how-a-soft-fork-might-establish-a-block-size-truce-or-not-1451423607. Visited on 15 Aug 2019

191. A. Van Wirdum, in *Bitcoin Magazine – The Power of Schnorr: The Signature Algorithm to Increase Bitcoin's Scale and Privacy, Apr 2016*, https://bitcoinmagazine.com/articles/the-power-of-schnorr-the-signature-algorithm-to-increase-bitcoin-s-scale-and-privacy-1460642496. Visited on 15 Aug 2019

192. M. von Haller Gronbaek, in *Blockchain 2.0, smart contracts and challenges*, Bird & Bird. (2016), https://www.twobirds.com/en/news/articles/2016/uk/blockchain-2-0--smart-contracts-and-challenges. Visited on 28 Oct 2017

193. *W3C – Decentralized Identifiers (DIDs) v1.0*, https://w3c.github.io/did-core/. Visited on 1 Dec 2019

194. *W3C – Leading the web to its full potential*, https://www.w3.org/. Visited on 1 Dec 2019

195. *W3C Credentials Community Group – DID Method Registry*, https://github.com/w3c-ccg/did-method-registry. Visited on 1 Dec 2019

196. *W3C Credentials Community Group – Sovrin DID Method Specification*, https://sovrin-foundation.github.io/sovrin/spec/did-method-spec-template.html. Visited on 1 Dec 2019

197. *W3C Credentials Community Group – DID Syntax*, https://w3c.github.io/did-core/#did-syntax. Visited on 1 Dec 2019

198. *Web of Trust Info – Decentralized Key Management System*, https://github.com/WebOfTrustInfo/rwot4-paris/blob/master/topics-and-advance-readings/dkms-decentralized-key-mgmt-system.md. Visited on 1 Dec 2019

199. *Wikipedia – Ghash.io*, https://en.wikipedia.org/wiki/Ghash.io. Visited on 01 Dec 2019

200. *Wikipedia – Nonce*, https://de.wikipedia.org/wiki/Nonce. Visited on 01 Dec 2019
201. *O. Wyman – Blockchain: The Backbone Of Digital Supply Chains*, http://www.oliverwyman. com/our-expertise/insights/2017/jun/blockchain-the-backbone-of-digital-supply-chains. html. Visited on 01 Dec 2019
202. *Zhaw – Was ist der Unterschied zwischen Microgrids und Smart Grids*, https://www.zhaw. ch/de/lsfm/institute-zentren/iunr/ecological-engineering/erneuerbare-energien/microgrids/ unterscheidung/. Visited on 01 Dec 2019

Index

© Springer Nature Switzerland AG 2021
T. Gayvoronskaya, C. Meinel, *Blockchain*,
https://doi.org/10.1007/978-3-030-61559-8

Printed in the United States
By Bookmasters